Society at a Glance: Asia/Pacific 2022

OECD

BETTER POLICIES FOR BETTER LIVES

This work is published under the responsibility of the Secretary-General of the OECD. The opinions expressed and arguments employed herein do not necessarily reflect the official views of the Member countries of the OECD.

This document, as well as any data and map included herein, are without prejudice to the status of or sovereignty over any territory, to the delimitation of international frontiers and boundaries and to the name of any territory, city or area.

Please cite this publication as:
OECD (2022), *Society at a Glance: Asia/Pacific 2022*, OECD Publishing, Paris, https://doi.org/10.1787/7ef894e5-en.

ISBN 978-92-64-56983-6 (print)
ISBN 978-92-64-50205-5 (pdf)
ISBN 978-92-64-31605-8 (HTML)
ISBN 978-92-64-84947-1 (epub)

Society at a Glance: Asia/Pacific
ISSN 2408-915X (print)
ISSN 2408-9168 (online)

Foreword

Society at a Glance: Asia/Pacific, the OECD's overview of social indicators for the region, presents evidence on social trends across countries in Asia and the Pacific.

Chapter 1 introduces this volume and provides readers with a guide to help them interpret OECD social indicators. The remainder of the publication presents the indicators in a standardised format: one page of figures and accompanying text, pointing the reader to sources and potential caveats with measurement issues. The indicators are grouped in five chapters: general context, self-sufficiency, equity, health and social cohesion. Each chapter holds five indicators, but the health section includes an additional indicator to illustrate recent trends in cases and deaths related to the COVID-19 pandemic.

A previous draft of this report was discussed at the annual meeting of social policy experts organised by the OECD/Korea policy centre virtually on 16 December 2021. The draft benefitted from comments by the different experts including: Ashish Kumar Aggarwal (India); Shaikh Shamsuddin Ahmed (Bangladesh); Florence Bonnet (ILO); Solongo Algaa (Mongolia); Hyeon-kyeong Kim and Su-jin Kim (Korea); Norma Binti Mansor (Malaysia); Yang Lixiong (China); Theany Choeurng (Cambodia); Junko Takezawa (Japan); Michiel Van Der Auwera (ADB); Peter Whiteford (Australian National University); Turro Wongkaren (Indonesia); and, Suk-myung Yun (Korea).

This report was prepared by Willem Adema, Pauline Fron and Yukiko Takei, while EunKyung Shin contributed to a previous draft. The contribution of data on Social Expenditure by Michiel Van Der Auwera (ADB) is gratefully acknowledged. Maxime Ladaique (Fertility) and Philippe Herve and Cécile Thoreau (International Migration) contributed to Chapter 2; Jonas Fluchtmann provided data on labour force participation for Chapter 3, Andrew Reilly provided data on pensions for Chapter 4, while Luca Lorenzoni and Michele Cecchini provided data and comments on Chapter 5. This report was prepared in the OECD Directorate for Employment, Labour and Social Affairs (ELS) under the leadership of Stefano Scarpetta (Director of ELS), Mark Pearson (Deputy Director of ELS), and Monika Queisser (Senior Counsellor and Head of Social Policy). The many colleagues who provided assistance include Liv Gudmundson, Lucy Hulett and Natalie Corry.

The online version of this publication, including all figures and data, can be accessed at http://oe.cd/sag-asia.

Table of contents

FIGURES

TABLES

Follow OECD Publications on:

http://twitter.com/OECD_Pubs

http://www.facebook.com/OECDPublications

http://www.linkedin.com/groups/OECD-Publications-4645871

http://www.youtube.com/oecdilibrary

http://www.oecd.org/oecddirect/

This book has...

StatLinks

A service that delivers Excel® files from the printed page!

Look for the *StatLinks* at the bottom of the tables or graphs in this book. To download the matching Excel® spreadsheet, just type the link into your Internet browser, starting with the *https://doi.org* prefix, or click on the link from the e-book edition.

Acronyms and conventional signs

Asia/Pacific countries and economies ISO codes

Armenia	ARM
Azerbaijan	AZE
Bangladesh	BGD
Bhutan	BTN
Brunei Darussalam	BRN
Cambodia	KHM
China	CHN
Fiji	FJI
Georgia	GEO
Hong Kong, China	HKG
India	IND
Indonesia	IDN
Kazakhstan	KAZ
Korea Democratic People's Republic (hereafter Korea DPR)	PRK
Kyrgyzstan	KGZ
Lao People's Democratic Republic (hereafter Lao PDR)	LAO
Macau, China	MAC
Malaysia	MYS
Maldives	MDV
Mongolia	MNG
Nepal	NPL
Pakistan	PAK
Papua New Guinea	PNG
Philippines	PHL
Samoa	WSM
Singapore	SGP
Sri Lanka	LKA
Tajikistan	TJK
Thailand	THA
Timor-Leste	TLS
Tonga	TON
Turkmenistan	TKM
Uzbekistan	UZB
Viet Nam	VNM

OECD Asia/Pacific countries ISO Codes

Australia	AUS
Japan	JPN
Korea	KOR
New Zealand	NZL

Asia/Pacific refers to all countries for which data are shown, including OECD members Australia, Japan, Korea and New Zealand when relevant.

Conventional signs

.. or n.a: Not available.

(↘) in the legend relates to the variable for which countries are ranked from left to right in decreasing order.

(↗) in the legend relates to the variable for which countries are ranked from left to right in increasing order.

Executive summary

Society at a Glance: Asia/Pacific 2022 presents 26 key indicators on general socio-economic context, self-sufficiency, equity, health and social cohesion for 38 countries and territories in Asia and the Pacific.

Economic growth across Asia and the Pacific was hit by the COVID-19 pandemic, but prospects for growth remain strong…

Real GDP growth across the Asia/Pacific region fell markedly with the outbreak of the COVID-19 pandemic in 2020: growth rates in real GDP fell from 6% to 2.3% in China, and India, Indonesia, Japan and Korea all recorded a decline in GDP for 2020. Growth in GDP bounced back in 2021, and is forecast to remain strong in 2022 and 2023. Annual growth rates for China, India and the Asean countries were all projected to be in excess of 5% for 2022 and 2023 (*Economic Outlook for Southeast Asia, China and India 2022*). However, the war in Ukraine is expected to reduce global economic growth by about 1% in 2022 (*OECD Economic Outlook, Interim Report March 2022*).

…and while strong growth has reduced extreme poverty, income gaps remain wide

Strong economic growth across Asia and the Pacific over the past 20 years has substantially reduced extreme poverty; the share of people living with incomes below USD 1.90 per day has fallen from over 22% in 2000 to just below 5% in 2019 on average across the Asia/Pacific region. The gap in the income distribution between the richest and the poorest 10% of the population in the Asia/Pacific economies has declined over time, but it remains twice as large as the average for OECD countries.

Public social expenditure remains low in Asia and the Pacific and its redistributive power is limited

Social protection systems are underdeveloped in most countries of the region. Public social expenditure across Asia and the Pacific was just 7% of GDP in 2018/9, compared with 20% of GDP, on average, in the OECD countries. The redistributive power of social spending is limited as most social benefits concern payments to (former) workers with a formal employment contracts – a group that is relatively well-off compared to those in the informal sector. Informal employment continues to prevail in Asia and the Pacific, and these workers do not have access to social insurance benefits.

Population ageing is a social policy challenge affecting many countries in the region

Population ageing is an another important policy challenge, particularly in North East Asia, where rapid increases in life expectancy and even more rapid declines in fertility have resulted in the fastest rates of population ageing in history. By 2060 it is estimated that at least 20% of the population in Asia/Pacific economies will be aged 65 or older. In Korea, this is projected to concern 40% of the population by 2060: the highest proportion of all countries in the region.

At present only one in three persons of retirement age is covered by mandatory pension schemes in the Asia/Pacific region. This means that the elderly in the region will have to rely more on family support to meet their needs than their peers in OECD countries. To prevent increases in old-age poverty the gaps in social protection systems need to be addressed soon.

OECD/Korea Policy Centre

The Joint OECD/Korea Policy Centre (www.oecdkorea.org) is an international co-operation organisation established by a Memorandum of Understanding between the OECD and the Government of the Republic of Korea. The Centre – officially opened in 2008 – results from the integration of four pre-existing OECD/Korea Centres, one of which was the Regional Centre on Health and Social Policy (RCHSP), established in 2005.

The major functions of the Centre are to research international standards and policies on international taxation, competition, public governance, and social and health policy sectors in OECD member economies and to disseminate research outcomes to public officials and experts in the region. In the area of health and social policy, the Centre promotes policy dialogue and information sharing between OECD economies and non-OECD Asian/Pacific countries.

There are four main areas of work: social protection statistics (jointly with the International Labour Organization and the Asian Development Bank); the Family Database for the Asia/Pacific region; health expenditure and financing statistics, quality of care indicators and policies to improve affordability of medicines (jointly with the World Health Organization) and on pension policies (jointly with the World Bank). In pursuit of this vision, the Centre hosts various kinds of educational programme, international meetings, seminars, and workshops in each sector and provides policy forums presented by experts at home and abroad.

1 Introduction to *Society at a Glance: Asia/Pacific*

Society at a Glance: Asia/Pacific provides an OECD overview of social indicators in the region. It provides quantitative evidence on social indicators, and presents internationally comparable data on a range of issues. The presented evidence include data on, economic growth, labour market participation, international migration, social expenditure, poverty and income inequality, demographic trends, pensions, marriage and divorce, early childhood education and care, educational attainment, health status, COVID-19 and health expenditure, social cohesion and life satisfaction.

The *Society at a Glance: Asia/Pacific* series provides an example of how OECD frameworks may be used to highlight and illustrate societal progress and social policy issues in the Asia/Pacific region (OECD, 2019[1]). The purpose of *Society at a Glance: Asia/Pacific* and the *Society at a Glance* series more generally[1] is to provide information on two questions:

- Compared with their own past and with other countries, what progress have countries made in their social development?
- How effective have been societies' efforts to further their own development?

Addressing the first question about societal progress requires indicators that cover a broad range of social outcomes across countries and over time. As social development requires improvements in health, education and economic resources, as well as a stable basis for social interactions, indicators have to be found for all these dimensions.

The second question about societal effectiveness is even more challenging to answer. Societies try to influence social outcomes, often through government policy. Whether policies are effective in achieving their aims is a critical issue. Indicators help to make that assessment. A first step is to compare the resources intended to change outcomes across countries and contrast those resources with social outcomes. While this comparison is far from being a comprehensive evaluation of policy effectiveness, indicators can contribute to highlighting areas where more evaluative work may be needed.

The framework of OECD social indicators

The structure applied here is not a full-scale framework of social indicators. But it is more than a simple list of indicators. This framework has been informed by experiences in other parts of the OECD on policy and outcome assessment in a variety of fields. It draws, in particular, on the OECD experience with environmental indicators. The indicators are based on a variant of the "Pressure-State-Response" (PSR) framework that has also been used in other policy areas (United Nations, 1996[2]). In this framework human activities exert **pressures** on the environment, which affect the **state** of natural resources and environmental conditions, and which prompt a **societal response** to these changes through various policies. The PSR framework highlights these sequential links, which in turn helps decision-makers and the public to interconnections that are often overlooked.

A similar approach for social indicators is followed in this report. Indicators are grouped along two dimensions their nature and the policy fields that they cover. The first dimension is broken down into three areas:

- **Social context** refers to variables that, while not usually direct policy targets, are crucial for understanding the social policy context. For example, the proportion of elderly people in the total population is not a policy target. However, it is relevant information about the social landscape in which, for example, health, taxation or pension policy responses are made. Unlike other indicators, trends in social context indicators cannot be unambiguously interpreted as "good" or "bad".
- **Social status** indicators describe the social outcomes that policies try to influence. These indicators describe the general conditions of the population. Ideally, the indicators chosen are ones that can be easily and unambiguously interpreted – all countries would rather have low poverty rates than high ones, for example.
- **Societal response** indicators provide information about what society is doing to affect social status indicators. Societal responses include indicators of government policy settings. Additionally, the activities of non-governmental organisations, families and the broader civil society also involve societal responses. Comparing societal response indicators with social status indicators provides an initial indication of policy effectiveness.

An important limitation of the social context, social status and societal response indicators used here is that these are presented at a national level. For countries with a significant degree of federalism and/or regional variation, Australia, China or India such indicators may not be reflective of the different regions within the federation, which may have different contexts, outcomes and social responses. This limitation should be borne in mind in considering the indicators presented below.

In addition, the framework used in *Society at a Glance: Asia/Pacific* groups "social status" and "social response" indicators according to the broad policy fields that they cover:

1. **Self-sufficiency** is an underlying objective of social policy. Self-sufficiency is promoted by ensuring people's active social and economic participation, and their autonomy in activities of daily life.

2. **Equity** is another longstanding objective of social policy. Equitable outcomes are measured mainly in terms of access by people and families to resources.

3. **Health** status is a fundamental objective of health care systems, but improving health status also requires a wider focus on its social determinants, making health a central objective of social policy.

4. **Social cohesion** is often identified as an over-arching objective of countries' social policies. While little agreement exists on what it means, a range of symptoms are informative about a lack of social cohesion. Social cohesion is more positively evident in the extent to which people participate in their communities.

The selection and description of indicators

Asia/Pacific countries differ substantially in the ways that they collect and publish social indicators. In selecting indicators for this report, the following questions were considered.

- What is the minimum degree of indicator comparability across countries? This report strives to present the best comparative information for each of the areas covered. However, the indicators presented are not confined to those for which there is "absolute" comparability. Readers are, however, alerted as to the nature of the data used and the limits to comparability.

- What is the minimum number of countries for which the data must be available? This report generally includes only indicators that are available for a majority of countries.

- What decompositions should be used at a country level? Social indicators can often be disaggregated at a national level into outcomes by social sub-categories, as for example people's age. Pragmatism prevails: the decompositions presented here vary according to the indicator considered. Individual indicators can be relevant for multiple areas of social policy. That is to say, they could plausibly be included under more than one category. For example, the ability to undertake activities of daily living without assistance is potentially an indicator of social cohesion, self-sufficiency and health. Indicators are presented here under the category for which they are considered to be most relevant.

General social context indicators

When comparing social status and societal response indicators, it is easy to suggest that one country is doing badly relative to others, or that another is spending a lot of money in a particular area compared with others. It is important to put such statements into a broader context. For example, national income levels vary across OECD countries. If there is any link between income and health, richer countries may have better health conditions than poor ones, irrespectively of societal responses. If the demand for health care services increases with income (as appears to be the case), rich countries may spend more on health care (as a percentage of national income) than poorer countries. These observations do not mean that the indicators of health status and health spending are misleading. They do mean, however, that the general context behind the data should be borne in mind when considering policy implications.

General social context indicators, including fertility, marriage and divorce, migration and the old age support ratio, provide the general background for the other indicators in this report. GDP per capita is a social outcome in its own right, giving an indication of the average material well-being of that society.

Table 1.1. List of general context indicators

GDP per capita
Fertility
Marriage and divorce
International migration
Old-age support ratio

Self-sufficiency indicators

For many people, paid active labour force participation and employment provide income, identity and social interactions. Hence promoting higher labour force participation and paid employment is a priority for most countries. A better education enables longer term self-sufficiency now and in the future, including in paid employment. Early childhood education provides a foundation for future learning, as well as freeing up mothers to choose to work. Educational attainment and students performance provides information on human capital accumulation. Education spending provides information on the primary social response made by governments to help ensure self-sufficiency. The reader should keep that these self-sufficiency indicators are also related to equity indicators, such as employment, pensions and social spending.

Table 1.2 List of self-sufficiency indicators

Social status	Societal responses
Labour force participation	Education spending
Employment	
Early childhood education and care	
Educational attainment and student performance	

Equity

Equity has many dimensions. It concerns the ability to access social services and economic opportunities, as well as equity in outcomes. Opinions vary widely as to what exactly entails a fair or a just distribution of opportunities. Additionally, as it is hard to obtain information on all dimensions of equity, the social status equity indicators are focussed on inequality in financial resources.

Table 1.3. List of equity indicators

Social status	Societal responses
Poverty	Pensions: coverage and replacement rates
Income inequality	Public social expenditure
	Solidarity

Poverty is a natural starting point for considering equity at the bottom of society. Absolute measures of poverty are used here, since many of the region's countries are very poor. In addition to an absolute poverty measure, an indicator of relative inequality across the distribution is also considered. Pension coverage and the old-age replacement rate are important indicators of the extent to which society treats its older people in an equitable fashion. Many Asia/Pacific countries have social protection systems that redistribute resources and insure people against various contingencies. These interventions are summarised by public social spending, while the solidarity indicator reflects on the extent to which people make donations and/or participate in voluntary work.

Health

The links between social and health conditions are strong. Indeed, educational gains, accompanied by public health measures, better access to health care and continuing progress in medical technology, have contributed to significant improvements in health status, as measured by life expectancy. To a significant extent, improvements in life expectancy reflect lower infant mortality. As it is essential for economic development and well-being to access sufficient, safe, nutritious food and balanced diet, child malnutrition is a salient indicator to predict a country's economic and social development potential.

Health expenditure is a general and key part of the policy response of health care systems to concerns about health conditions. The indicator on hospital activities provides information on the number of hospital beds, discharge rates and duration of stays in hospitals. Nevertheless, health problems are frequently rooted in interrelated social conditions – such as unemployment, poverty and inadequate housing – that are beyond the reach of health policies.

Table 1.4. List of health indicators

Social status	Societal responses
Life expectancy	Health expenditure
Neonatal, infant and child mortality	Hospital activities
Child malnutrition	
COVID-19	

Social cohesion

Promoting social cohesion is an important social policy goal in many countries. However, because there is no commonly-accepted definition, identifying suitable indicators is particularly difficult. The approach taken here in *Society at a Glance: Asia/Pacific* is to assess social cohesion through indicators that describe the extent to which citizens participate in societal life trust their fellow citizens and institutions, and derive satisfaction from their daily activities.

Table 1.5. List of social cohesion indicators

Social status	Societal responses
Life satisfaction	
Confidence in institutions	
Trust and safety	
Tolerance	
Voting	

Life satisfaction is strongly associated with confidence in the broader society and its institutions. A general measure of trust in other people and safety may indicate the degree to which economic and social exchange is facilitated, enhancing well-being and facilitating socially productive collective action. The degree of community acceptance of minority groups (migrants, ethnic minorities and gay and lesbian people) is a measurable dimension of social cohesion. Finally, high voter turnout indicates that a country's political system enjoys a high level of participation, increasing its effectiveness and reflecting a broad public consensus about its legitimacy.

What can be found in this publication?

Chapters 2 to 6 cover each of the five domains of social indicators as discussed above. For each indicator, there is a page of text and a page of figures. Both figures and text are, to a degree, standardised. Both the text and figures address the most recent headline indicator data, with country performances often ranked from best to worst. Changes in the indicator over time and the length of the time-period at hand can be considered when data are available. Having addressed the indicator and changes over time, the text and figures then typically consider an alternative disaggregation of the indicator, or relationships with other social outcomes or policies. For each indicator, a boxed section on "Definition and measurement" provides the definitions of the data used and a discussion of potential measurement issues. Finally, suggestions for further reading can be given.

References

OECD (2020), *How's Life? 2020: Measuring Well-being*, OECD Publishing, Paris, [3] https://doi.org/10.1787/9870c393-en.

OECD (2019), *Society at a Glance: Asia/Pacific 2019*, OECD Publishing, Paris, [1] https://doi.org/10.1787/soc_aag-2019-en.

United Nations (1996), "Glossary of Environment Statistics", *F*, No. 67, Department for Economic [2] and Social Information and Policy Analysis, Studies in Methods, https://unstats.un.org/unsd/publication/SeriesF/SeriesF_67E.pdf (accessed on 29 November 2018).

Note

[1] A related OECD publication, *How's life? 2020: Measuring Well-being*, (OECD, 2020[3]) presents the latest evidence from over 80 indicators, covering both current well-being outcomes and resources for future well-being, and including changes since 2010. Compared with *Society at a Glance*, it uses a broader set of outcome measures but does not include indicators of policy responses.

2 General context indicators

GDP per capita

Gross domestic product per person (GDP per capita) varies considerably across the Asia/Pacific region (Figure 2.1). Differences in GDP per capita within the Asia/Pacific region are large: Singapore's GDP per capita is more than 25 times higher than GDP per capita in Tajikistan and Timor-Leste. GDP per capita is well above the OECD average (USD 44 800) in the richest economies in the region: Australia, Brunei Darussalam, Hong Kong, China (China) and Singapore. By contrast, more than two-thirds of the Asia/Pacific have a GDP per capita that is below the regional average (USD 19 900).

Real GDP growth for the Asia/Pacific region fell markedly at the beginning of the COVID-19 pandemic, in 2020 (Figure 2.2). Growth in GDP bounced back in 2021, and is forecast to remain strong in 2022, even though growth rates will abate somewhat. The growth rate in China in 2022 is forecast to be slightly lower than in 2018-19, just before the outbreak of the COVID-19 pandemic, while in Japan the growth in GPD per capita is forecast to be somewhat higher in 2022 than in 2018-19.

Across the Asia/Pacific region, the annual average growth rate of GDP per capita over the 2015-20 period (1.4%) was slightly higher than previously (0.9% between 2012 and 2017). This rise is largely related to substantially increased growth rates some countries during the 2015-20 period, in particular Bangladesh, Tajikistan and Viet Nam (Figure 2.3).

Evidence on "catch-up" and GDP convergence is weak among countries in the Asia/Pacific region (Figure 2.3). There is hardly any negative correlation between the pace of growth in GDP per capita over the period 2015-20 and the initial level in 2015. OECD countries in the region have relatively high GDP per capita and recorded slow annual growth over this five-year period. However, many poorer countries in the Asia/Pacific region recorded a similar pace in growth since 2015. GDP per capita in China and Turkmenistan increased more rapidly than one might have expected given its level in 2015.

Definition and measurement

Among the different measures available in the System of National Accounts (SNA), gross domestic product (GDP) per capita is the one most commonly used for comparing the sizes of across countries. GDP per capita measures the sum of marketed goods and services produced within the national boundary, averaged across everyone who lives within this territory.

GDP per capita is calculated using a country's GDP in 2020 the United States dollars (USD) which is then divided by the country's total population. Real annual average growth is calculated using a country's GDP per capita in constant 2010 USD as compound annual growth rate during the period (2015-20). Level log of GDP per capita is calculated by using common log for the GDP per capital of the reference year (2015).

The data come from the World Bank, World Development Indicators (World Bank, 2021[1]).

Reference

World Bank (2021), *World Development Indicators*, https://databank.worldbank.org/source/world-development-indicators#. [1]

Figure 2.1. GDP per capita varies considerably across the Asia/Pacific region

Current GDP per capita (↘), 2020 (2020 USD)

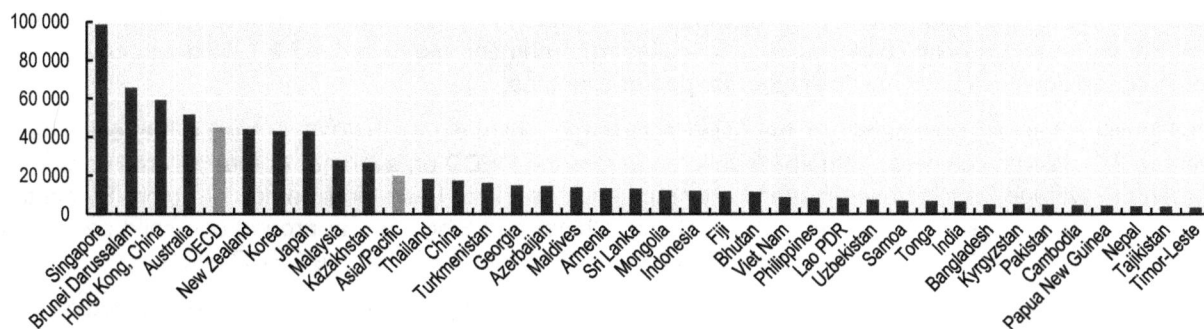

Source: OECD National Accounts Database (2021); World Bank (2021), World Development Indicators.

StatLink ☰ https://stat.link/hvwydg

Figure 2.2. Countries experienced a decline in GDP growth with the outbreak of the COVID-19 pandemic

Real GDP growth in selected countries, percentage change from previous years

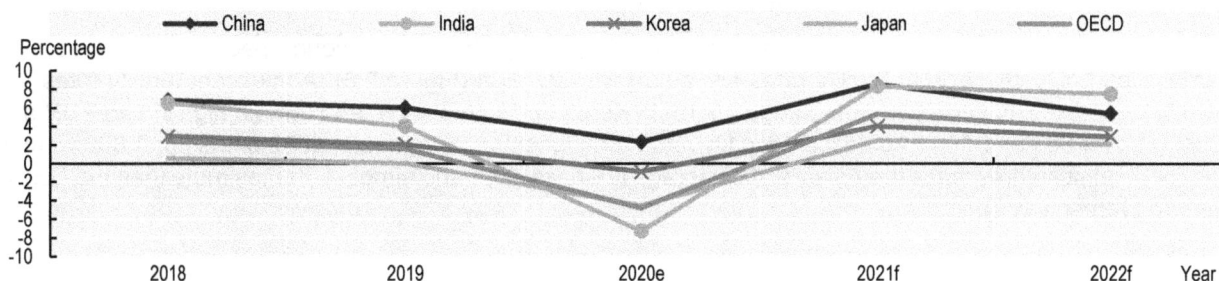

Note: e = estimate; f = forecast.
Source: World Bank (2021), World Development Indicators.

StatLink ☰ https://stat.link/sf4l86

Figure 2.3. Evidence on "catch-up" and GDP convergence is weak among countries in the Asia/Pacific region

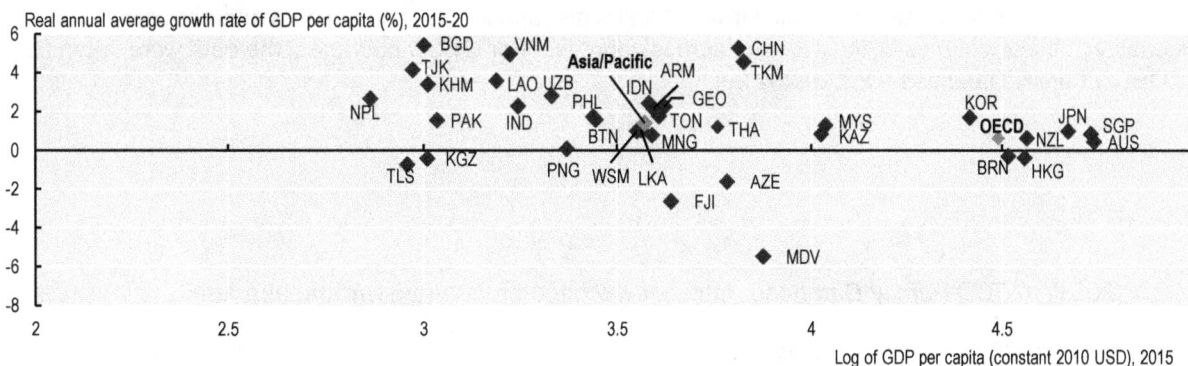

Source: World Bank (2021), World Development Indicators.

StatLink ☰ https://stat.link/5ztmuh

Fertility

The total fertility rate (TFR) gives an indication of the number of children an average woman will have in her lifetime. The size of the population remains stable if the total fertility rate is a little over two, allowing for some mortality during infancy and childhood. This so-called "replacement rate" is around 2.1 children per women for industrialised countries but it may be higher for poorer countries.

Total fertility rates vary considerably in the Asia/Pacific region (Figure 2.4). In 2019, women in the region had on average 2.3 children compared with at 1.6 children across the OECD on average. At four children or more per women on average, fertility rates in island countries such as Timor-Leste and Samoa are high. By contrast, fertility rates are lowest in Korea, Hong Kong, China (China) and Singapore at around one child per woman. Japan, Thailand and Macau, China (China) all also have TFRs that are below the OECD average.

Birth rates have declined sharply over the past decades. The TFR average across the Asia/Pacific region fell by almost 3 children per woman from 1970 to 2019. OECD member countries in the region, with the exception of Korea, experienced a slower decline in the TFR at less than 1.5 children per woman on average. The Maldives recorded the largest decline in the TFR, from over seven children per woman in 1970 to 1.8 in 2019. No country had higher TFRs in 2019 than in 1970. Kazakhstan, Kyrgyzstan, Georgia and Mongolia are the only economies which had higher TFRs in 2019 than in 1995.

Women in poor economies have much higher fertility rates than women in wealthier economies (Figure 2.5). In 2019, women in OECD and East Asian economies had the fewest children compared with the greater Asia/Pacific region. As more women gain higher educational attainment and pursue labour market careers, they tend to postpone having children and/or have fewer children altogether.

In countries where birth rates for adolescent girls are high – and where many young people are married (see Marriage and divorce), overall fertility rates are also relatively high (Figure 2.6). Adolescent fertility rates are lowest (around 1 child per 1 000 women age 15-19) in Korea and Korea DPR, and remain high in Lao PDR and Nepal (at over 60 per 1 000). Adolescent fertility rates are highest in Bangladesh at 82 births per 1 000 women age 15-19, almost three times the Asia/Pacific average (29 per 1 000) and almost six times more than the OECD average (14 per 1 000).

Definition and measurement

The total fertility rate (TFR) in a specific year corresponds to the number of children that would be born to each woman if she were to live to the end of her childbearing years and if the likelihood of her giving birth to children at each life stage followed the currently prevailing age-specific fertility rates. The adolescent fertility rate is defined as the annual number of births per 1 000 women age 15 to 19.

The data presented here are extracted from the World Bank's World Development Indicators which for population data uses the United Nations Population Statistics as its key source (http://esa.un.org/wpp). These population statistics are based on administrative "vital registration" data, census data and/or survey data, and the quality of these sources is likely to vary across countries. For OECD countries, the data were taken from the OECD Family Database (OECD, 2021[1]).

References

OECD (2021), *OECD Family Database*, https://www.oecd.org/els/family/database.htm. [1]

United Nations (2019), *World Fertility Data 2019*, [2]
https://www.un.org/development/desa/pd/data/world-fertility-data.

Figure 2.4. Despite rapid declines, fertility rates in Asia/Pacific are still higher than in OECD

Number of children per woman aged 15 to 49, in 1970, 1995 and 2019 or nearest year

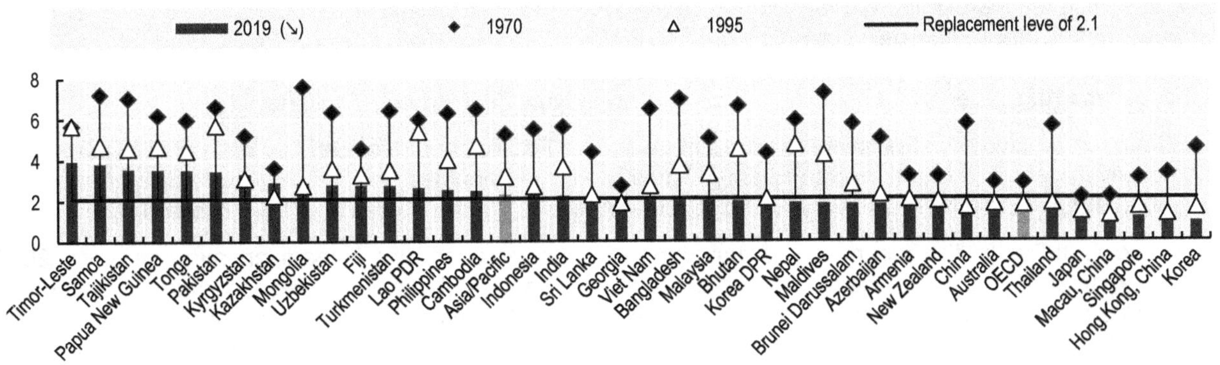

Legend: ■ 2019 (↘)   ◆ 1970   △ 1995   — Replacement leve of 2.1

Countries (x-axis): Timor-Leste, Samoa, Tajikistan, Papua New Guinea, Tonga, Pakistan, Kyrgyzstan, Kazakhstan, Mongolia, Uzbekistan, Fiji, Turkmenistan, Lao PDR, Philippines, Cambodia, Asia/Pacific, Indonesia, India, Sri Lanka, Georgia, Viet Nam, Bangladesh, Malaysia, Bhutan, Korea DPR, Nepal, Maldives, Brunei Darussalam, Azerbaijan, Armenia, New Zealand, China, Australia, OECD, Thailand, Japan, Macau, China, Singapore, Hong Kong, China, Korea

Source: World Bank (2021), World Development Indicators; for OECD countries OECD Family Database (2021).

StatLink ⬛ https://stat.link/me3yfv

Figure 2.5. Richer countries have lower fertility rates

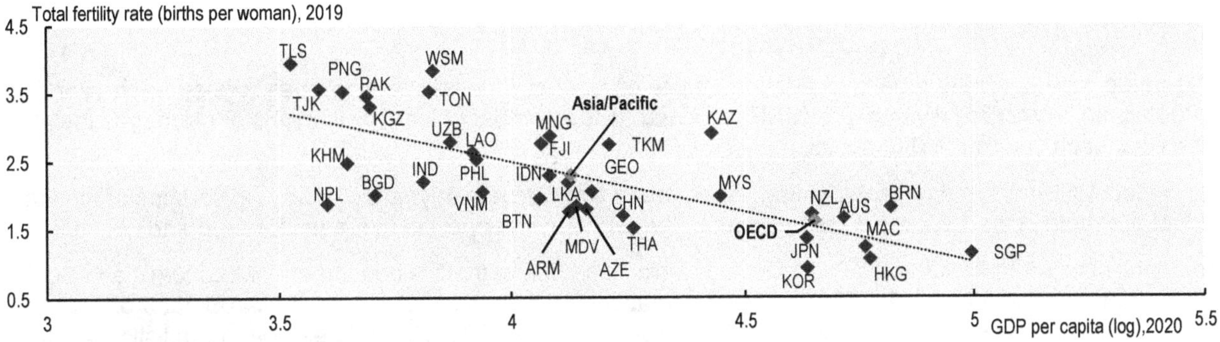

Total fertility rate (births per woman), 2019

Labels: TLS, PNG, WSM, PAK, TJK, TON, KGZ, UZB, LAO, MNG, Asia/Pacific, KAZ, FJI, TKM, KHM, IND, GEO, BGD, PHL, IDN, MYS, NZL, BRN, NPL, VNM, LKA, CHN, AUS, MAC, BTN, OECD, JPN, HKG, SGP, ARM, MDV, THA, AZE, KOR

X-axis: GDP per capita (log), 2020

Source: World Bank (2021), World Development Indicators; for OECD countries OECD Family Database (2021).

StatLink ⬛ https://stat.link/mdr07l

Figure 2.6. Countries with high fertility rates tend to also have high adolescent birth rates

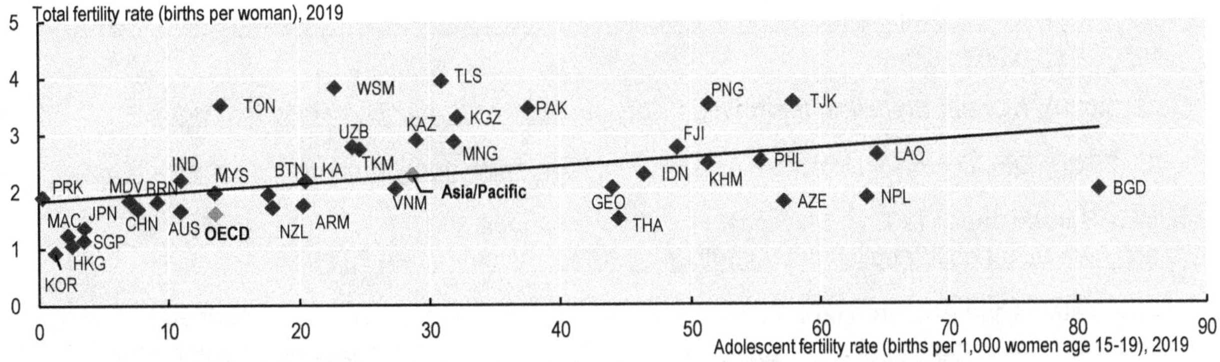

Total fertility rate (births per woman), 2019

Labels: WSM, TLS, TON, PNG, TJK, KAZ, KGZ, PAK, UZB, MNG, FJI, IND, MYS, BTN, LKA, TKM, PHL, LAO, PRK, MDV, BRN, VNM, Asia/Pacific, IDN, KHM, BGD, MAC, JPN, CHN, GEO, AZE, NPL, SGP, AUS, OECD, NZL, ARM, THA, HKG, KOR

X-axis: Adolescent fertility rate (births per 1,000 women age 15-19), 2019

Source: World Bank (2021), World Development Indicators; for OECD countries OECD Family Database (2021).

StatLink ⬛ https://stat.link/ixfec5

Marriage and divorce

Both marriage and divorce rates have increased in the Asia/Pacific region since 2005 (Figure 2.7 and Figure 2.8). The increase in the crude marriage rate across Asia/Pacific was limited, but it contributed to crude marriage rates in the region being almost 1.5 times higher than the average across OECD countries. Crude marriage rates are highest at over nine marriages per 1 000 adults in Fiji, Tajikistan and Uzbekistan; they are around four marriages per 1 000 adults in Australia, Korea, New Zealand and Thailand.

Since 2005, crude divorce rates have increased in most Asia/Pacific countries – and by around 25% across the region on average, while crude divorce rates in China more than doubled. In contrast, crude divorce rates fell among the OECD countries in the Asia/Pacific region – Australia, Japan, Korea and New Zealand.

Across the Asia/Pacific the mean age of first marriage has increased by 3 years on average since 2005 (Figure 2.9). In 2005, the mean age at first marriage across the selected Asia/Pacific economies was 24.0 years for women and 27.4 years for men. By 2019, the mean age at first marriage had increased to 27.5 years for women and to 30.1 years for men, still some 3 to 3.5 years below the OECD average for men and women. A strong tendency of postponing marriages is observed across Asia/Pacific economies, but large cross-national differences remain: since 2005, the mean age at first marriage has increased by about four years among men and women in Armenia, while change was much more limited in New Zealand and Singapore where the mean age of first marriage for men increased by less than a year. Only in Viet Nam, is the mean age for women in 2019 slightly lower than in 2005.

Definition and measurement

The crude marriage rate is defined as the number of legal civil unions or marriages formed each year per 1 000 adults. The crude divorce rate (CDR), defined as the number of legal civil unions or marriages that are dissolved each year per 1 000 adults.

The mean age at first marriage is defined as the mean average age in years of marrying persons at the time of first marriage. This measure is disaggregated by gender with separate averages for men and women.

The data were taken from the 2019 UN Demographic Yearbook of the UN department of Economic and Social Affairs Statistics Division (2019[1]), OECD Family Database Asia Pacific (2021[2]), Australian Bureau of Statistics (2020[3]), Statistics New Zealand (2020[4]), Statistics Bureau Japan (2021[5]), and Korea's official statistics (2020[6]).

References

Australian Bureau of Statistics (2020), *Marriages and Divorces, Australia*, [3]
https://www.abs.gov.au/statistics/people/people-and-communities/marriages-and-divorces-australia/latest-release.

KOSIS (2020), *KOrean Statistical Information Service*, https://kosis.kr/search/search.do. [6]

OECD (2021), *OECD Family Database Asia/Pacific*, http://www.oecdkorea.org/user/nd8662.do. [2]

Statistics Bureau Japan (2021), *Statistical Handbook of Japan 2021*, [5]
https://www.stat.go.jp/english/data/handbook/pdf/2021all.pdf#page=23.

Stats NZ Tatauranga Aotearoa (2020), *Marriages, civil unions, and divorces: Year ended* [4]
December 2020, https://www.stats.govt.nz/information-releases/marriages-civil-unions-and-divorces-year-ended-december-2020.

UN Demographic Yearbook (2019), *Demographic and Social Statistics*, [1]
https://unstats.un.org/unsd/demographic-social/products/dyb/dyb_2019/.

Figure 2.7. Trends in marriage rates vary across countries
Crude marriage rates, per 1 000 persons, 2005 and 2019 or the latest year

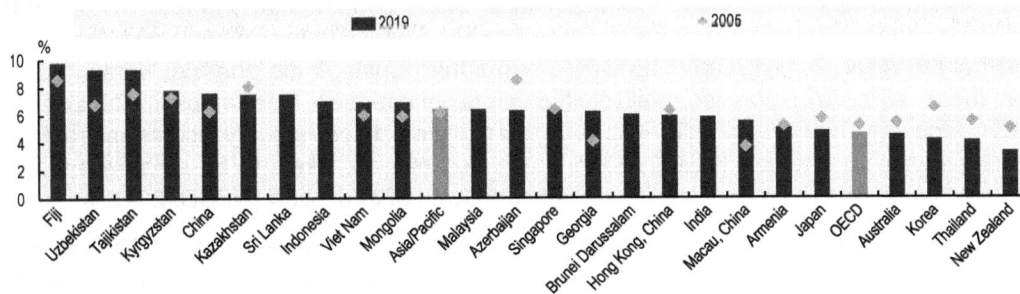

Note : Data refer to 2019 except for Korea, Mongolia, New Zealand and Thailand (2020), Armenia, Azerbaijan, Brunei Darussalam, Georgia, India, Kyrgyzstan, Malaysia, and Tajikistan (2018), Indonesia (2016) and Fiji (2014). The OECD average is the unweighted average across the 34 OECD countries with data available.
Source: United Nations (2019), UN Demographic Yearbook 2019; OECD (2021), OECD Family Database Asia Pacific (China, Indonesia, Mongolia, Thailand and Viet Nam); Australian Bureau of Statistics (2020), Marriages and Divorces; Stats NZ Tatauranga Aotearoa (2020), Marriages, civil unions, and divorces, December 2020; Statistics Bureau Japan (2021), Statistical Handbook of Japan 2021; KOSIS Korean Statistical Information Service (2020), Crude Divorce Rate 2020.

StatLink ᵐˢᴾ https://stat.link/nvxb3o

Figure 2.8. Except for OECD countries, divorce rates generally increased across the Asia/Pacific region since 2005
Crude divorce rates, per 1 000 persons, 2005 and 2019 or the latest year

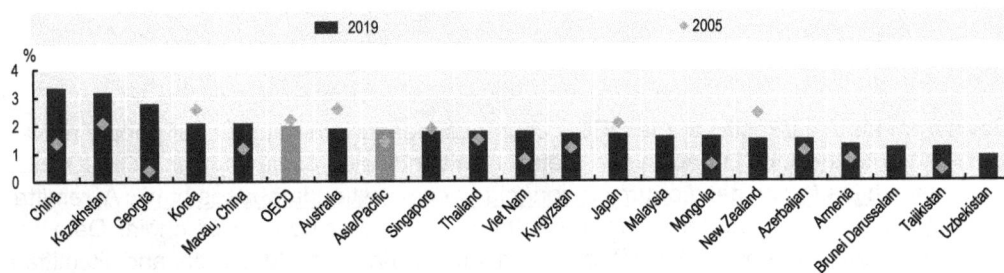

Note: Data refer to 2019 except for Korea, Mongolia and Thailand (2020) and Armenia, Azerbaijan, Brunei Darussalam, Georgia, Kyrgyzstan, Malaysia, and Tajikistan (2018). The OECD average is the unweighted average across the 36 OECD countries with data available.
Source: United Nations (2019), UN Demographic Yearbook 2019; OECD (2021), OECD Family Database Asia Pacific (China, Mongolia, Thailand and Viet Nam); Australian Bureau of Statistics (2020), Marriages and Divorces; Stats NZ Tatauranga Aotearoa (2020), Marriages, civil unions, and divorces, December 2020; Statistics Bureau Japan (2021), Statistical Handbook of Japan 2021; KOSIS Korean Statistical Information Service (2020), Crude Divorce Rate 2020; other countries, OECD (2021), OECD Family Database.

StatLink ᵐˢᴾ https://stat.link/izhm2j

Figure 2.9. The mean age of first marriage has increased since 2005
The mean age of first marriage, 2005 and 2019 or the latest year

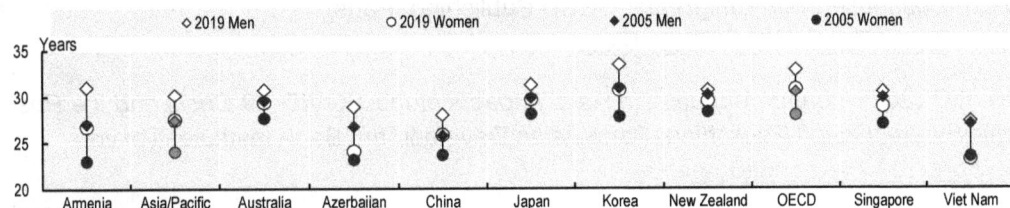

Note: Data for Armenia and Singapore refer to 2018 and 2020 respectively.
Source: Eurostat (2021), (Armenia and Azerbaijan); OECD (2021), OECD Family Database Asia Pacific (China, Korea, Mongolia, and Viet Nam); Australian Bureau of Statistics (2020), Marriages and Divorces; Statistics Singapore (2020), Statistics on Marriages and Divorces, 2020 (Singapore); Stats NZ Tatauranga Aotearoa (2020), Marriages, civil unions, and divorces, December 2020; Statistics Bureau Japan (2021), Statistical Handbook of Japan 2021; KOSIS Korean Statistical Information Service (2020), Crude Divorce Rate 2020; other countries, OECD (2021), OECD Family Database.

StatLink ᵐˢᴾ https://stat.link/c5lvu6

International migration

The share of migrant flows from the Asia/Pacific region to OECD countries among total inflows to the OECD (around 29%) is unchanged, even though the absolute number doubled between 2000 and 2019 (Figure 2.10). More than half of the Asian immigrants to the OECD came from China, India and Viet Nam in 2019. In 2019, migrants from the Asia/Pacific region had relatively high employment rates, for example in Canada (73.3%), the EU 28 (65.8%), and the United States (71.4%), but the situation differs sharply across migrant groups and countries of origin within the region (OECD, 2015[1]). Women are less likely to be employed than men, and employment rates of migrants increase significantly with the level of education (OECD, 2015[1]).

The deployment of labour migrants decreased drastically across the Asia/Pacific region in 2020, due to the huge impact of the COVID-19 pandemic (Figure 2.11). Especially in the beginning of the pandemic, worker deployments were suddenly suspended and barely picked up at the end of 2020. For example, in Bangladesh, the outflow of workers dropped to almost zero for months and did not significantly resume before December 2020. In Indonesia, it started to recover earlier than in Bangladesh, but in both countries, the end-of-year level was below half of what it was in December 2019 (OECD/ADBI/ILO, 2021[2]).

Remittance flows to Asia and the Pacific have continuously increased since 2000, but not in 2020 because of the COVID-19 pandemic. Of all remittances sent to Asian/Pacific countries in 2020, more than half went to India (27%), China (19%), and the Philippines (11%) (Figure 2.12). Remittances sent by Asian/Pacific migrants to their countries of origin amounted to USD 311 billion in 2020, accounting for more than two-thirds of all global remittance flows (USD 700 billion). Remittances constitute a significant share of gross domestic product in some of the countries of origin, as, for example, in Kyrgyzstan (29%), Nepal (24%), Tajikistan (27%) and Tonga (38%).

Definition and measurement

Immigrant flows from the Asia/Pacific to the OECD countries measure the number of people move from the Asia/Pacific countries to the OECD each year. Data on this indicator come from the OECD International Migration Database (https://www.oecd.org/migration/mig/oecdmigrationdatabases.htm). A remittance is a transfer of money by a foreign worker to an individual in his or her country of origin. Data on migrant remittance inflows in current (nominal) USD are from the World Bank Migration and Remittance Data (https://www.worldbank.org/en/topic/migrationremittancesdiasporaissues/brief/migration-remittances-data) (Figure 2.12).

References

OECD (2021), *International Migration Outlook 2021*, OECD Publishing, Paris, https://doi.org/10.1787/29f23e9d-en. [3]

OECD (2015), *Connecting with Emigrants*, OECD Publishing, Paris, https://doi.org/10.1787/9789264239845-en. [1]

OECD/ADBI/ILO (2021), *Labor Migration in Asia: Impacts of the COVID-19 Crisis and the Post-Pandemic Future*, OECD Publishing, Paris/Asian Development Bank Institute, Tokyo, https://doi.org/10.1787/a5d6e6aa-en. [2]

Figure 2.10. Migrant flows from Asia/Pacific to the OECD increased 2.5 fold since 2000

Inflows of foreign population by nationality (thousands)

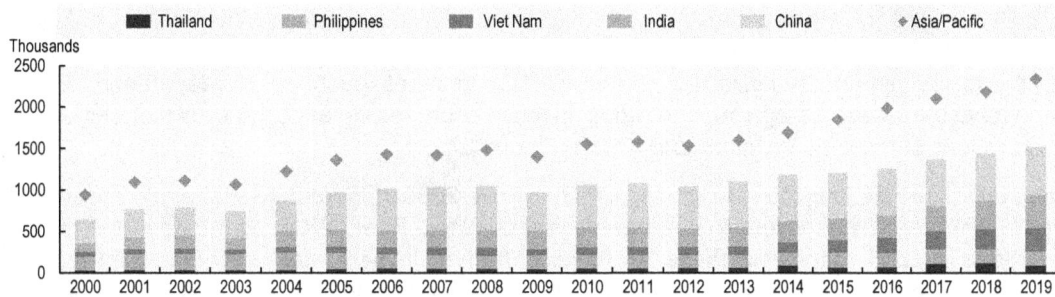

Note: Total of Asia/Pacific refers only to the countries available.
Source: OECD (2021), OECD International Migration Database.

StatLink 🔢 https://stat.link/y3io8t

Figure 2.11. The outbreak of the COVID-19 pandemic sharply reduced the outflow of workers

Monthly outflow of workers in Indonesia and Bangladesh in 2019 and 2020

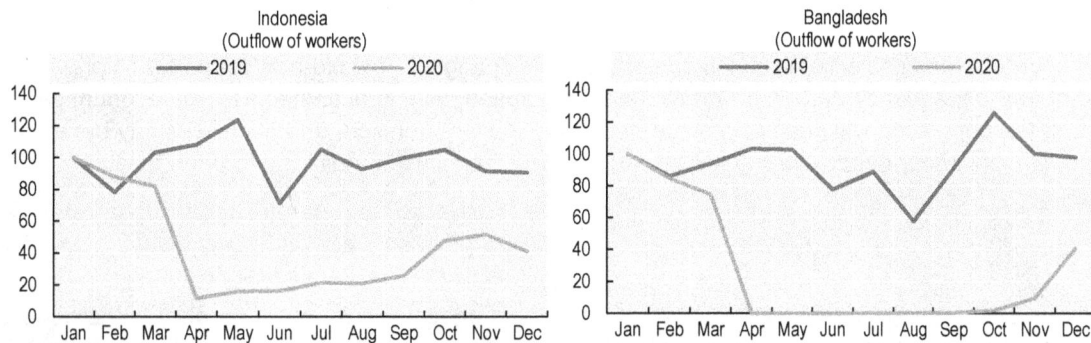

Source: OECD/ADBI/ILO (2021), *Labour Migration in Asia: Impacts of the COVID-19 Crisis and the Post-Pandemic Future.*

StatLink 🔢 https://stat.link/r2oe1q

Figure 2.12. Over half of migration remittance flows in Asia/Pacific went to India, China and the Philippines in 2020

Migrant remittance inflows to Asia/Pacific economies (USD billion)

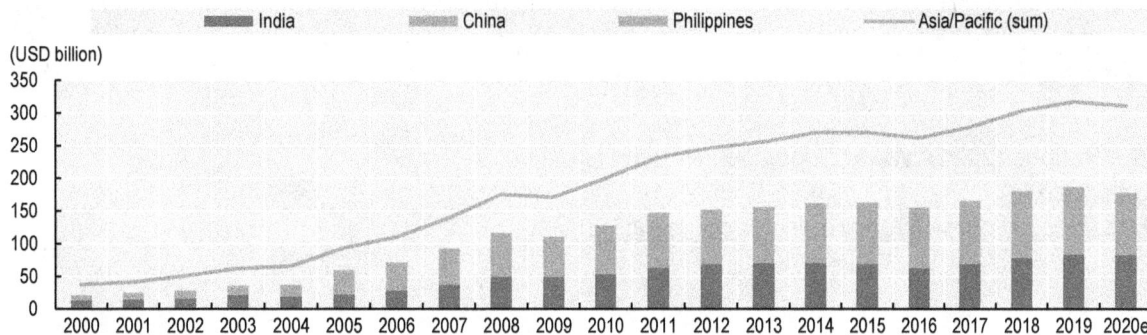

Note: 2020 data are estimates.
Source: World Bank (2021) Migration Remittances Data (May 2021 version).

StatLink 🔢 https://stat.link/knims0

Old-age support ratio

In 2020, countries in the Asia/Pacific region on average had ten people of working age for every person over 65 (Figure 2.13 Panel A). This is more than twice as high as the OECD average. The Maldives, Tajikistan and Papua New Guinea top the list with at least 17 working-age persons per one person over 65: a stark contrast to Japan's 1:2 ratio. Within the Asia/Pacific region, OECD countries such as Korea, Japan, Australia and New Zealand have the lowest old-age support ratios: in these countries life expectancy is high (Figure 5.1), while fertility rates are low, particularly in Japan and Korea (Figure 2.4).

Old-age support ratios are projected to more than halve by 2060 (Figure 2.13 Panel B), and the Maldives, Mongolia and Tajikistan are expected to see the biggest declines. Four OECD countries in the region already have low old-age support ratios and these will decline further, in particular in Korea, from 4.5 in 2020 to 1.2 persons of working age to 1 senior citizen in 2060. Other economies in the region will also experience rapidly ageing societies. For example, the old-age support ratio in Brunei Darussalam will decrease from 12.9 in 2020 to 2.4 in 2060, and in Hong Kong, China (China) and Singapore, the old-age support ratios are projected to fall to 1.4 and 1.5 respectively by 2060, well below the OECD average of 2.0.

The upward trend in elderly population stems from a rise in life expectancy due to improved health and declining birth rates. Underlying projected demographic trends do differ across countries (Figure 2.14), but the proportion of people aged 65 and over is estimated to at least double in most economies between 2020 and 2060. By 2060 it is estimated that at least 20% of the population in Asia/Pacific economies will be aged 65 or older. By 2060 over 40% of the population in Korea is estimated to 65 or older, the highest proportion of all countries in the region.

There are economic and social implications of demographic change. A low old-age support ratio provides some indication of the "dependency burden on the working population, as it is assumed that the economically active proportion of the population will need to provide health, education, pension, and social security benefits for the inactive population, either directly through family support mechanisms or indirectly through taxation.

Data and measurement

The "old-age support ratio" relates the number of individuals aged 15 to 64 (working age) to the population aged 65 and over (those of "pension age"). All ratios are presented as the number of working age (15-64) people per one non-active person. The old-age support ratio thus provides a rough indicator of the number of active people who potentially are economically and socially supporting elderly people. It also gives a broad indication of the age structure of the population. Changes in the support ratio depend on mortality and fertility rates and, to a much lesser degree, on net migration.

Data come from the United Nations' World Population Prospects online database (2021[1]), The projections for population aged 65 used in this section are based on the "medium variant" population projections.

Reference

United Nations (2021), *World Population Prospects online database*, [1]
http://esa.un.org/wpp/unpp/panel_population.htm.

Figure 2.13. The old-age support ratio will more than halve across the Asia/Pacific region

A. Old age support ratio, 2020
Number of the population aged 15-64 per member of the population aged 65+

B. Decline in the old-age support ratio
Old-age support ratio, 2020 and 2060
■ 2060   ▫ Difference 2020-2000

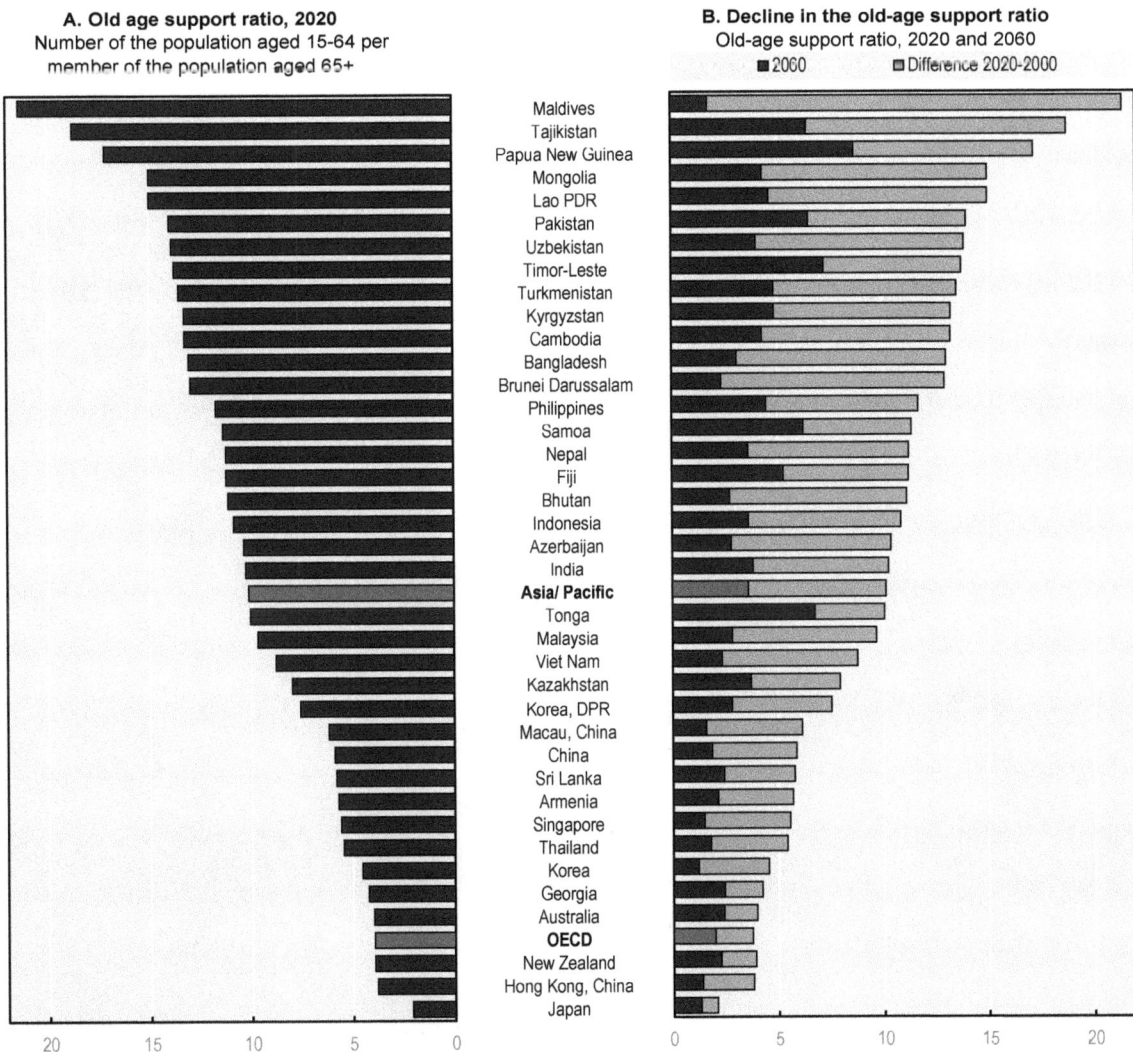

Note: The old-age support ratio is defined as the number of the population aged 15-64 per member of the population aged 65+.
Source: UN World Population Prospects (2019), 2019 Revision.

StatLink https://stat.link/587aic

Figure 2.14. Populations are ageing across the region

Projected percentage of population aged 65 and over in selected countries, 2020-60

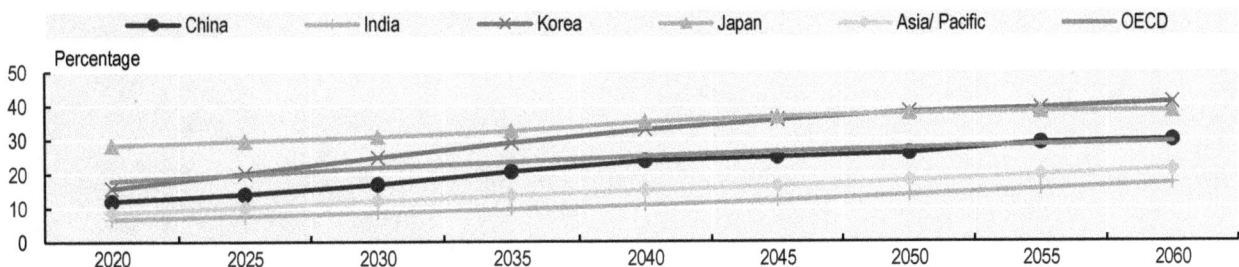

Source: UN World Population Prospects (2019), 2019 Revision.

StatLink https://stat.link/a5mpjl

3 Self-sufficiency

Labour force participation

Labour force participation rates in 2019 were on average somewhat lower in OECD countries (61.4%) than in Asia/Pacific countries (63.2%), (see Figure 3.1). In 2019, the highest labour force participation rates were recorded for Nepal, Cambodia and Korea DPR at over 80%, while these were below 50% in India, Papua New Guinea, Tonga, Samoa and Tajikistan.

There is a gender gap in labour force participation rates. On average across the region labour force participation rates were 74% for men and 53% for women in 2019. In that year, gender labour force participation rate gaps exceeded 40 percentage points in Bangladesh, India, the Maldives and Sri Lanka, and at 60 percentage points was largest in Pakistan. The smallest gender gaps in favour of men (1 to 2 percentage points) were recorded for Papua New Guinea – where labour force partition rates were 47% and Nepal, which with 82.5% recorded the highest labour force participation rate of the region.

Looking ahead, OECD projections (Figure 3.2) show that – if male and female labour participation rates by five-year age groups follow the "baseline" scenario – the labour force will decrease substantially in Japan (from peak of 67 million in 2019), China (from peak of 805 million in 2020) and Korea (from peak of 28.3 million in 2025). In contrast, Australia, India and Indonesia are projected to experience an increase in the size of the labour force over the next few decades. G20 countries have committed to reduce the gender gap in labour force participation rates. This scenario would have a significant effect on the size of the labour force in several countries, especially in India, where female labour force participation rates are currently low, the labour force could potentially double by 2060.

Definition and measurement

The labour force participation rate is a measure of the proportion of a country's working-age population (15 and more) that engages actively in the labour market, either by working or looking for work for at least one hour in the reference week. It provides the relative size of the supply of labour available to engage in the production of goods and services. Data was taken from the ILO's Key Indicators of the Labour Market (KILM) database for non-OECD countries.

The labour force projections presented here are based on population projections for persons aged 15-74 years and current rates of labour market entry and exit. The model is a dynamic age-cohort model that projects future labour participation by gender and five-year age group. Three scenarios are considered, and based on OECD population data and the OECD Employment Database.

1. Baseline: In many countries, there has been an increase trend in the participation of women which has offset a decline in participation rates for men, and there have been different trends by age. Rather than assuming fixed participation rates, the baseline scenario uses current (2011-20) rates of labour market entry and exit to project participation rates by gender and five-year age group over the period to 2060.

2. Gender gap reduced by 25% by 2040, and halved by 2060: Male participation rates are held at the baseline, with female participation rates projected such that the gender participation gap in 2025 is 25% smaller than the gap in 2020, and the gap in 2040 50% smaller than in 2020.

3. Gender gap halved by 2040, and closed by 2060: Male participation rates are held at the baseline, with female participation rates projected such that the gender participation gap in 2040 is 50% smaller than the gap observed in 2020, and is closed completely by 2060.

Figure 3.1. There is a gender gap in labour force participation in favour of men in all countries

Labour force participation by gender, 2019

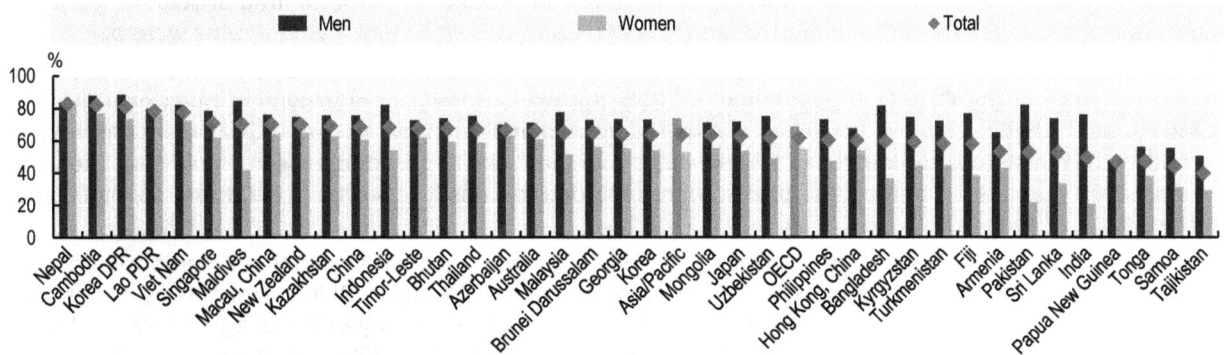

Source: International Labour Organization (2020), ILOSTAT Labour force participation rate (%) by sex and age, November 2020.

StatLink ⬛ℹ️ https://stat.link/qyo0bh

Figure 3.2. Labour force projections, selected countries, 2020-60

Projected number of persons aged 15-74 in the labour force, thousands

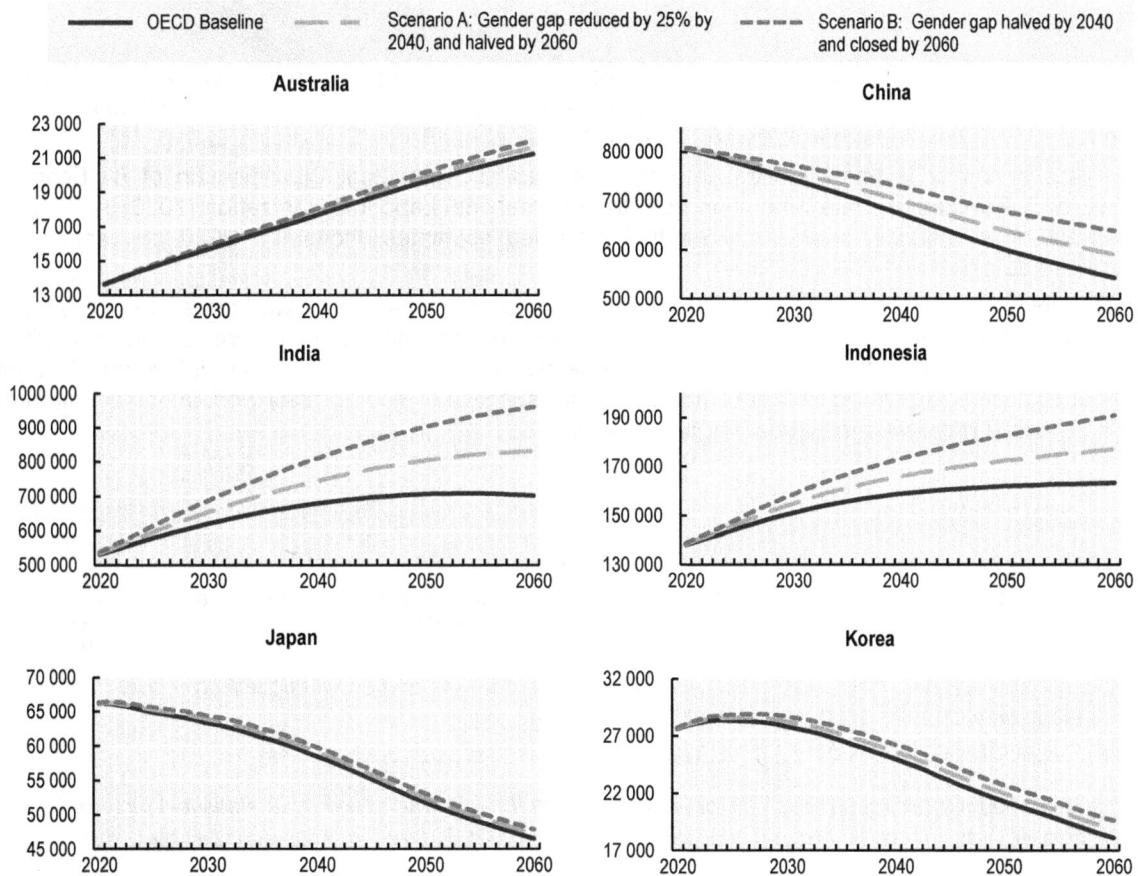

Note: The labour force projections are based on population projections for persons aged 15-74 years, by five-year age groups, and labour force participation data from the OECD.

Source: OECD Secretariat calculations based on OECD population data and the OECD Employment Database.

StatLink ⬛ℹ️ https://stat.link/sgazuf

Employment

Employment is a key factor in self-sufficiency. On average, almost 60% of the population over age 15 were employed in Asia/Pacific (58.5%) and OECD countries (55.9%) in 2020 (Figure 3.3). In that year, employment rates were in excess of 75% in Cambodia, Korea DPR and Lao PDR, while employment rates were below 40% in Samoa and Tajikistan.

With the outbreak of the COVID-19 pandemic in 2020, the upward trend in employment rates over the past decade came to a halt in many countries in the Asia/Pacific region. Employment rates in 2020 were below those recorded in 2011 in about three-quarters of Asia/Pacific countries. The largest decrease in employment between 2011 and 2020 – above 7.0 percentage points, were recorded for mostly low-employment rate countries such as Armenia, India, Kyrgyzstan and Tonga.

People in high-income economies are more likely to work in the non-agricultural sector compared with those in low-income economies (Figure 3.4). Over 80% of people employed Macau, China, Hong Kong, China, and Singapore are engaged in the service-sector with less than 0.5% of all employed in the agricultural sector. By contrast, the largest share of employed people in Lao PDR and Nepal – over 60%, are in the agricultural sector.

Informal employment prevails in Asia/Pacific economies (Figure 3.5). More than 80% workers in the non-agricultural sector are engaged in informal employment in Cambodia, Bangladesh, India, Indonesia, Lao PDR, Nepal and Pakistan. Gender gaps in informal employment are small. Women in countries in South Asia such as Bangladesh, Pakistan, and India are more likely to be in informal employment in the non-agricultural sector than men, but men are more likely to be involved in informal employment in countries that were part of the former Soviet Union, such as Armenia, Kyrgyzstan and Georgia.

Definition and measurement

The employment rate is defined as the ratio of employed people over age 15 to the population over age 15 for the data taken from the International Labour Organization's ILOSTAT database for non-OECD countries, and the four OECD countries refer to by age total in OECD Labour Force Statistics (2020[1]).

Employment by sector is based on the International Standard Industrial Classification of All Economic Activities (ISIC Revision 4). Data was taken from the International Labour Organization (2020[2]), ILOSTAT, Employment by sex and economic activity; ILO modelled estimates, November 2020 (thousands) and calculated as percentage.

Informal employment is defined by the nature of the enterprise: own-account workers and employers are having the informal employment status when the job has the informal sector nature. Employers, with or without hired workers, operating an informal enterprise are classified as in informal employment. All family workers are classified as having informal employment, irrespective of whether they work in formal or informal sector enterprises (International Labour Organization, 2018[3]).

References

International Labor Organization (2021), *The Contribution of Social Dialogue to Gender Equality*, https://labordoc.ilo.org/permalink/41ILO_INST/j3q9on/alma995111793202676. [4]

International Labor Organization (2020), *ILOSTAT, Employment by sex and economic activity -- ILO modelled estimates, Nov. 2020 (thousands)*, https://www.ilo.org/ilostat-files/Documents/Excel/INDICATOR/EMP_2EMP_SEX_ECO_NB_A_EN.xlsx. [2]

International Labour Organization (2018), *Women and men in the informal economy: a statistical picture (third edition)*, https://www.ilo.org/global/publications/books/WCMS_626831/lang--en/index.htm. [3]

OECD (2020), *OECD Labour Force Statistics 2020*, OECD Publishing, Paris, https://doi.org/10.1787/5842cc7f-en. [1]

Figure 3.3. About 60% of the population over age 15 are employed in Asia/Pacific economies

Share of employed people over age 15 to the population over age 15 (%), 2011 and 2020 or the latest year

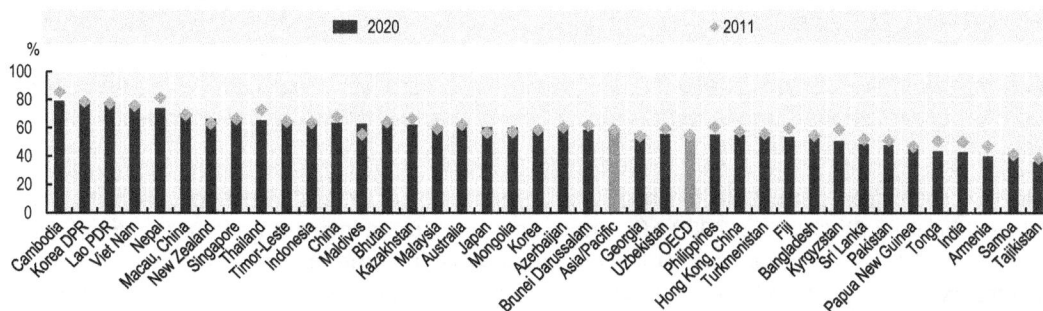

Note: The data in ILOSTAT database refers to the employment rate by age 15 and over, and for the data in OECD database refer to by age total.
Source: OECD (2020), OECD Labour Force statistics for OECD countries as well as OECD average; and International Labour Organization (2020), ILOSTAT Employment to population ratio – ILO modelled estimates (%) for other countries.

StatLink https://stat.link/ympnw2

Figure 3.4. People in high-income economies are more likely to work in the non-agricultural sector

Employment by sector, ILO modelled estimates (%), 2019

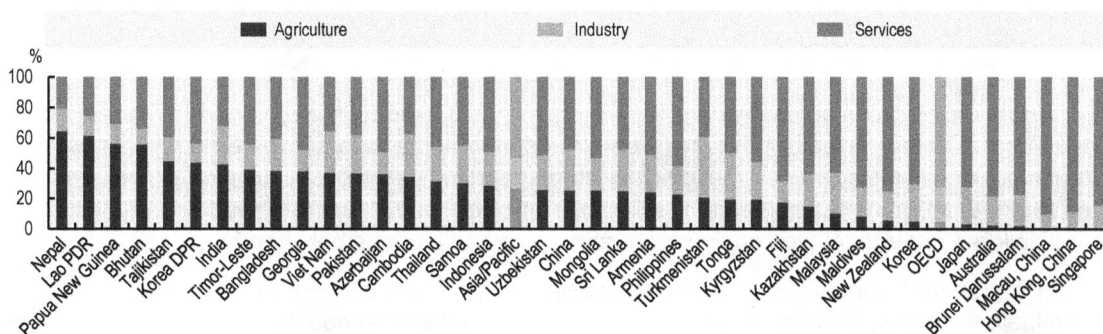

Source: International Labour Organization (2020), ILOSTAT, Employment by sex and economic activity; ILO modelled estimates, November 2020 (thousands).

StatLink https://stat.link/dz8esw

Figure 3.5. Informal employment prevails in Asia/Pacific economies

Share of informal employment in non-agricultural employment by sex (%), 2020 or the latest year

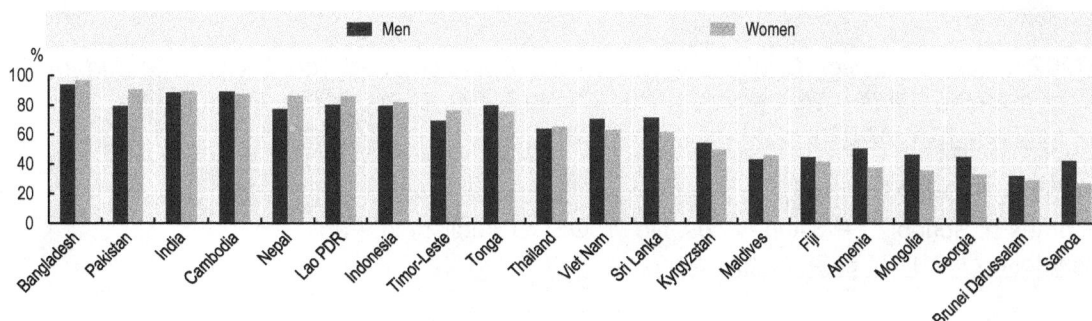

Source: International Labour Organization (2020), ILOSTAT, Informal employment rate by sex (%/ annual).

StatLink https://stat.link/btcokn

Early childhood education and care

Public support for early childhood education and care (ECEC) services helps achieve a range of policy goals. Public investment in ECEC simultaneously enhances child development and helps children acquire the necessary skills to support their future lives, while it also supports parents in their daily quest to balance work and family commitments. As women traditionally engage most in care work, such supports particularly facilitate female labour force participation and are thus crucial to achieving greater gender equality in employment participation.

The extent to which children participate in pre-primary education (often children age 3 to 5 inclusive) varies across countries (Figure 3.6). Over the 2009-19 period, enrolment rates in pre-primary education in Asia/Pacific economies increased steadily in about half of the countries while in some others greater gains were recorded. Pre-primary enrolment ratios tripled in Bangladesh and Lao PDR, and doubled in Timor-Leste and Kyrgyzstan. Gender gaps in ECEC participation are small (Figure 3.7). Girls in Georgia, Malaysia, Maldives and Sri Lanka are more likely to participate in ECEC services than boys, but boys are more likely to attend ECEC programmes in Bhutan, Nepal and Pakistan.

Results of the OECD Programme for International Student Assessment (PISA) have shown that 15-year-old students who had attended pre-primary education perform better on PISA tests than those who did not, even after accounting for their socio-economic backgrounds (OECD, 2011[1]). For the few countries in the region for which data is available, higher rates of ECEC participation in 2009 are associated with higher score of the 2018 OECD PISA reading and mathematics assessment (Figure 3.8).

Definition and measurement

World Bank data on the gross enrolment rate for pre-primary, are used for the early childhood education and care (ECEC) participation indicator. The gross enrolment ratio is the ratio of total enrolment, regardless of age, to the population of the age group that officially corresponds to the level of education shown. Pre-primary education refers to programmes at the initial stage of organised instruction, designed primarily to introduce very young children to a school-type environment and to provide a bridge between home and school.

The OECD Programme for International Student Assessment (PISA) is a triennial international survey, which aims to evaluate education systems worldwide by testing the skills and knowledge of 15-year-old students. The data was taken from the OECD PISA 2018 Database.

The employment rate is defined as the ratio of employed people over age 15 to the population over age 15. Data was taken from the International Labour Organization's Key Indicators of the Labour Market (LILM) Database for non-OECD countries and the OECD Employment Database for the Four OECD countries.

References

OECD (2020), *Building a High-Quality Early Childhood Education and Care Workforce: Further Results from the Starting Strong Survey 2018*, TALIS, OECD Publishing, Paris, https://doi.org/10.1787/b90bba3d-en. [2]

OECD (2011), "Does Participation in Pre-Primary Education Translate into Better Learning Outcomes at School?", *PISA in Focus*, No. 1, OECD Publishing, Paris, https://doi.org/10.1787/5k9h362tpvxp-en. [1]

Figure 3.6. Enrolment in pre-primary education in Asia/Pacific economies is increasing

Gross enrolment ratio of pre-primary education, total, percentage, 2009 and 2019 or the latest year

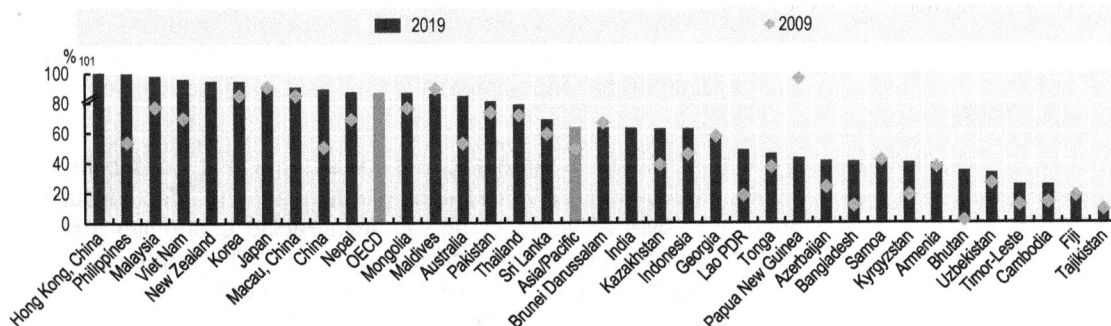

Source: OECD countries refer to OECD (2021), Enrolment rates in pre-primary education or primary school; children aged three to five year old. Other countries refer to World Bank (2021), World Development Indicators.

StatLink https://stat.link/a8wbkl

Figure 3.7. Gender gaps in pre-primary education participation are small

Gross enrolment ratio of pre-primary education, boys and girls, percentage, 2019 or the latest year

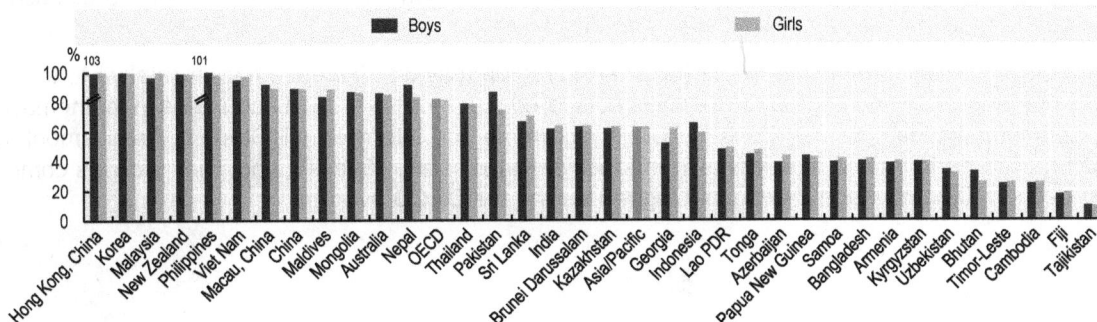

Source: OECD countries refer to OECD (2021), *Education at a Glance 2021*. Other countries refer to World Bank (2021), World Development Indicators.

StatLink https://stat.link/icl64w

Figure 3.8. Higher rates of pre-primary education participation are associated with higher PISA scores

Gross enrolment ratio of pre-primary education of 2009 (%), total (X-axis) and the 2018 mean PISA score (Y-axis)

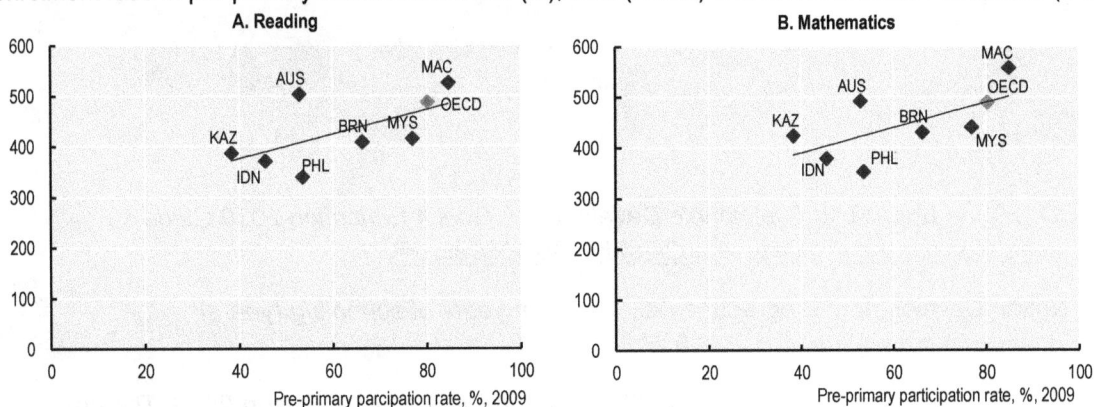

Source: World Bank (2021), World Development Indicators; OECD (2018), PISA 2018 database.

StatLink https://stat.link/kaz1ce

Educational attainment and student performance

The level of education of the population gives an indication of its stock and quality of human resources. A higher stock and quality of human resources may mean higher labour productivity and hence a higher income-generating capacity. The average number of years spent in education among the working-age population is the most readily available and cross-nationally comparable measure of educational attainment across the Asia/Pacific region.

The United Nation Sustainable Development Goal 4.1 targets to ensure all girls and boys complete free, equitable and quality primary and secondary education (12 years) leading to relevant and effective outcomes by 2030. However, on average, the population over 25 years of age in Asia/Pacific economies has been in education for almost nine years with large cross-national differences (Figure 3.9). The population over 25 in Australia, Georgia, Japan, and New Zealand spent more years in education than the OECD average (12 years), while in some countries – Bhutan, Cambodia, Nepal, Pakistan, Papua New Guinea and Timor-Leste – the number of years spent in education is below five years on average. There is a gender gap in educational attainment in Asia/Pacific economies in favour of men. In 2019, men over 25 in Asia/Pacific economies spent on average 0.6 years more in education than women: this gender gap in mean years of schooling is significantly wider in India (3.3 years) and Pakistan (2.5 years).

Trends over the past decade, suggest that the average years of schooling of those aged 25 and over increased across both OECD and Asia/Pacific economies (Figure 3.10). Especially, the Maldives, Malaysia and Pakistan are rapidly increasing the average level of educational attainment. Over the 2005-19 period, many countries including Armenia, Sri Lanka and the Maldives – have been closing the gender gap in mean years of schooling, while the gender gap increased in Kazakhstan and Timor-Leste.

Future educational attainment levels in the Asia/Pacific region may well increase further relative to the OECD. Students from Singapore and large Chinese cities outscored students from OECD countries in mathematics and reading competency tests of the 2018 OECD Programme for International Student Assessment (PISA) (Figure 3.11). The performance of students in Indonesia, Kazakhstan, Malaysia and Thailand was comparable with their peers in Colombia and Mexico, but lagged behind the OECD average.

Definition and measurement

Mean years of schooling measure average number of years of education received by people ages 25 and older, converted from education attainment levels using official durations of each level ((United Nation Development Programme, 2021[1]). Data on the average years of education is taken from Human Development Indices and Indicators based on UNESCO Institute for Statistics (2020), Barro and Lee (2018), ICF Macro Demographic and Health Surveys, UNICEF Multiple Indicator Cluster Surveys and OECD (2019).

The OECD programme for International Student Assessment (PISA) data was taken from the OECD PISA 2018 Database.

References

UNESCO (2017), *Unpacking Sustainable Development Goal 4 Education 2030 Guide*, http://unesdoc.unesco.org/images/0024/002463/246300E.pdf. [2]

United Nation Development Programme (2021), *Mean years of schooling (years)*, http://hdr.undp.org/en/indicators/103006. [1]

United Nation Development Programme (2020), *Human Development Report 2020; The next frontier-Human development and the Anthropocene*, http://hdr.undp.org/sites/default/files/hdr2020.pdf. [3]

Figure 3.9. On average across the Asia/Pacific region, adults have had about 9 years of schooling

Mean years of schooling, people aged 25 and older in 2019

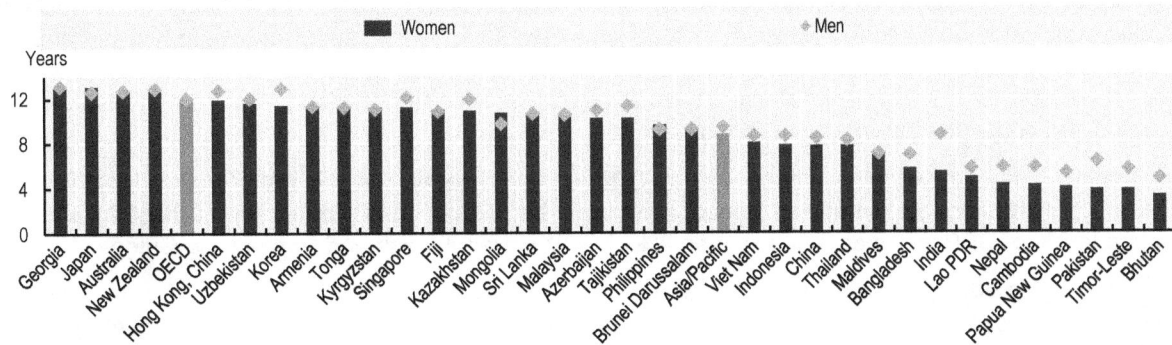

Source: United Nation Development Programme (2021), Human Development Reports.

StatLink https://stat.link/bgsafh

Figure 3.10. The average years in schooling increased across the Asia/Pacific region over the past decade

Change in mean years of total schooling (2005-19)

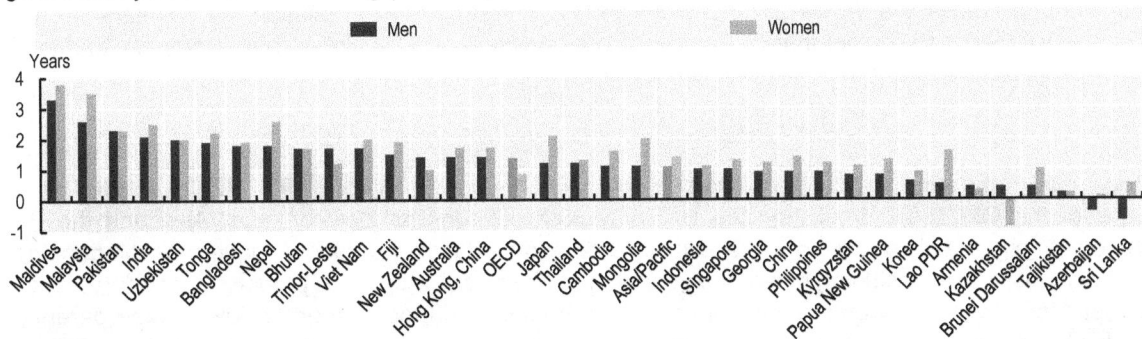

Source: United Nation Development Programme (2021), Human Development Reports.

StatLink https://stat.link/r6ylwt

Figure 3.11. Students from some Asia/Pacific cities and countries outscored the average OECD student

Mean Score of PISA 2018 results (Reading and Mathematics) in selected countries

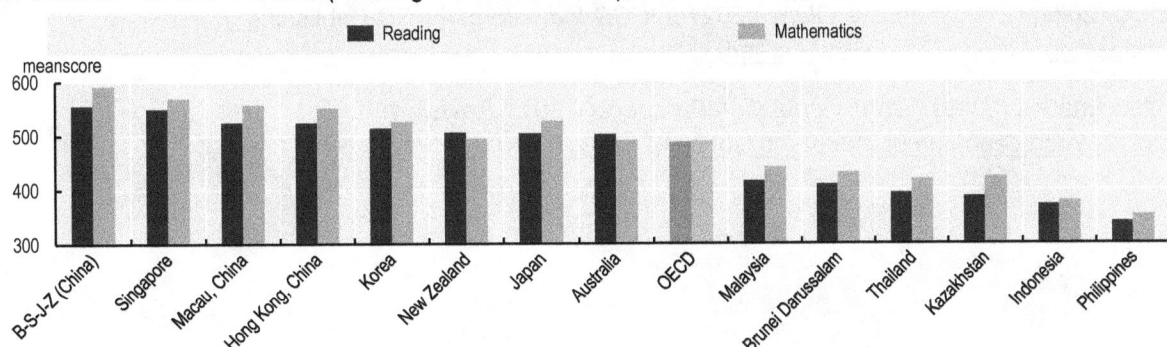

Note: B-S-J-Z (China) refers to the four PISA participating China provinces: Beijing, Shanghai, Jiangsu, and Zhejiang.
Source: OECD (2018), Program for International Student Assessment (PISA).

StatLink https://stat.link/1xi26k

Education spending

Public spending on education reflects society's investment in children to equip them with fundamental social and economic skills needed to be self-sufficient in their lives. Investing in education reduces poverty and boosts economic growth through human capital development, and is most efficient, in terms of long-term costs and benefits to society, and effective, in terms of human capital development, when investment starts during the early years and continues throughout childhood.

Public spending on education is around 4% of GDP on average across the Asia/Pacific and the OECD (Figure 3.12). However, cross-national variation is considerable. In 2020, public investment in education amounted to 8% of GDP in Tonga, but less than 2% of GDP in Bangladesh and Papua New Guinea.

Public spending on education as a percentage of GDP can be higher in richer countries than in poorer countries but this is not necessarily so (Figure 3.13). For example, public spending on education as a percentage of GDP is similar in Australia, Georgia, Korea, Mongolia, Samoa and Uzbekistan, at very different levels of GDP per capita (Chapter 2). These differences can be explained by a range of factors, such as the role of private financing of education, which in Korea is among the highest in OECD countries, the level of wages of educators, costs of education material, and also population structures (Chapter 2). For example, the proportion of children (0-19) in the populations of Mongolia and Samoa (38% and 47% respectively) is much higher than in Australia (25%) or Korea (17%).

When considering education spending per student the picture is different. Public spending on education per primary student is higher in richer countries (Figure 3.14) in the OECD on average it is more than twice as high as on average across the Asia/Pacific region. Public investment in education per student in Nepal is comparatively low, but still higher than in Cambodia (KHM) where GDP is higher than in Nepal (Chapter 2).

Data and measurement

Data on public education spending as a percentage of GDP were taken from OECD (2021[1]) Education at a Glance for the OECD countries, and the UNESCO Institute for Statistics for other Asia and the Pacific countries (http://data.uis.unesco.org/). Public spending on education includes government spending on educational institutions including different levels of education as pre-primary, primary, secondary education and post-secondary education and tertiary education, spending on fee support for low-income parents and towards school meals is included. Data on public spending per primary education student (in USD PPP) were taken from the UNESCO Institute for Statistics.

References

OECD (2021), *Education at a Glance 2021: OECD Indicators*, OECD Publishing, Paris, [1] https://doi.org/10.1787/b35a14e5-en.

United Nations (2019), *World Population Prospects - 2019 Revision*, [2] https://population.un.org/wpp/Publications/Files/WPP2019_Highlights.pdf.

Figure 3.12. Public investment in education increased across Asia Pacific countries

Public expenditure on education as percentage of GDP in 2010 and 2020

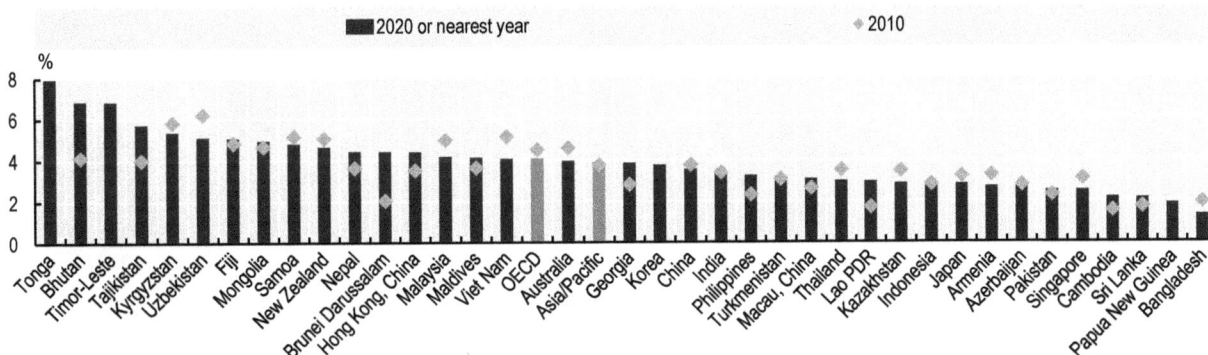

Note: Data refers to 2010 except for New Zealand and Turkmenistan (2012), Bangladesh (2009) and Samoa (2008). Data refers to 2020 except Tonga, Tajikistan, Kyrgyzstan, Fiji, Mongolia, Malaysia, Maldives, Viet Nam, the Philippines, Turkmenistan, Macau, China (China), Thailand, Kazakhstan, Indonesia, Azerbaijan, Pakistan and Bangladesh (2019); Bhutan, Timor-Leste, New Zealand, Nepal, Australia, Korea, China, Japan, Cambodia, Sri Lanka and Papua New Guinea (2018); Brunei Darussalam and India (2016); and Lao PDR (2014).
Source: UNESCO Institute for Statistics (2021), Government expenditure on education as a percentage of GDP http://data.uis.unesco.org/; OECD (2021), Education at a Glance 2021: Educational finance indicators for OECD countries. https://doi.org/10.1787/edu-data-en.

StatLink https://stat.link/bpfawl

Figure 3.13. Rich countries do not necessary spend more on education

Public expenditure on education as % of GDP, 2020 or nearest year

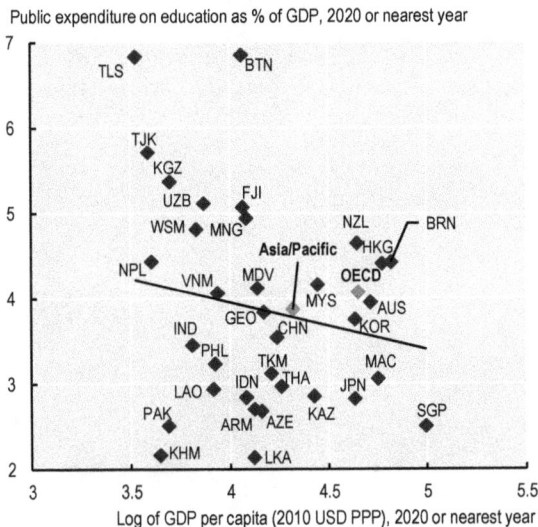

Source: UNESCO Institute for Statistics, Finance Indicators by ISCED level, http://data.uis.unesco.org/; OECD (2021) Education at a Glance 2021: Educational finance indicators, https://doi.org/10.1787/500dc1b1-en.

StatLink https://stat.link/51n8ai

Figure 3.14. Education as percentage of GDP and public spending per primary student

Initial government funding per primary student, constant PPP USD, 2020

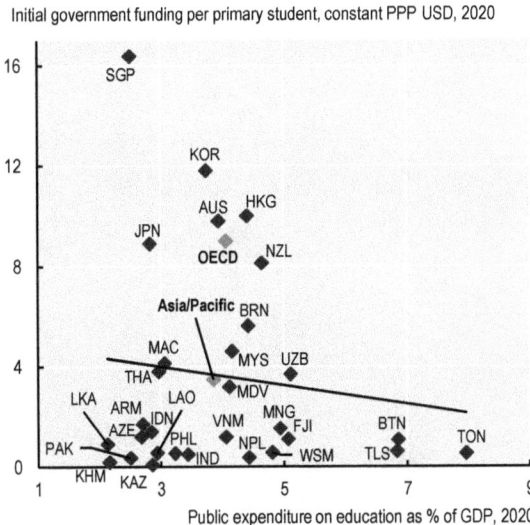

Source: UNESCO Institute for Statistics, Finance Indicators by ISCED level, http://data.uis.unesco.org/; OECD (2021) Education at a Glance 2021: Educational finance indicators, https://doi.org/10.1787/500dc1b1-en.

StatLink https://stat.link/s9gzae

4 Equity

Poverty

There has been marked progress on reducing extreme poverty over the past two decades: the share of people living in extreme poverty – with incomes below USD 1.90 per day, has fallen from over 22% in 2000 to just below 5% in 2019 across the Asia/Pacific region on average (Figure 4.1). Much of the observed reduction was driven by remarkable progress in China, Indonesia, Kyrgyzstan, Nepal, Tajikistan and Viet Nam, where poverty rates decreased by more than 30 percentage points.

Despite progress, extreme poverty is still widespread in India and Timor-Leste, where more than 20% of the population have to get by with less than USD 1.90 per day. Among low- and middle-income countries, poverty levels are lowest in China, Fiji, Mongolia and Thailand, where less than 0.5% of the population experiences severe poverty.

Poverty rates are a measure of inability to satisfy subsistence needs, including nutritional needs and prevention of communicable diseases. The number of deaths attributable to communicable diseases, maternal and prenatal conditions, and undernourishment is generally correlated with the share of the population living under the USD 1.90 poverty line (Figure 4.2). However, in Pakistan and the Philippines, the share of deaths by these factors is well above what one would expect given poverty rates. Lao PDR, Nepal and Timor-Leste also recorded a quite high number of deaths. In these countries, social policies may take on a greater focus on food security and public health.

Poverty generally declined more rapidly in countries with the strongest GDP growth (Figure 4.3). The pace of both economic growth and poverty reduction was fastest in Armenia, China and Viet Nam over the 2000-19 period. In contrast, in Lao PDR and Georgia the share of the population under the poverty line did not decline as much as one would have expected given the pace of economic growth.

Definition and measurement

Poverty rates are commonly measured by using income or consumption levels. The poverty rate is a headcount of how many people fall below the poverty line. Extreme poverty is defined as living on less than USD 1.90 a day per person, measured in 2011 Purchasing Power Parity prices (World Bank, 2021[1]). The United Nation Sustainable Development Goal 1 aims to end poverty in all its forms everywhere by 2030.

The indicator also presents information on cause of death refers to the share of all deaths for all ages by underlying causes. Communicable diseases and maternal, prenatal and nutrition conditions include infectious and parasitic diseases, respiratory infections, and nutritional deficiencies such as underweight and stunting.

GDP per capita is calculated using a country's GDP in the United States dollars (USD) which is then divided by the country's total population. Real annual average growth are calculated by using compound annual growth rate during the period (2000-20).

References

World Bank (2021), *World Development Indicators*, https://databank.worldbank.org.　[1]

World Bank (2020), *Poverty and Shared Prosperity 2020, Reversals of Fortune*,　[2]
https://openknowledge.worldbank.org/bitstream/handle/10986/34496/978146481
6024.pdf.

Figure 4.1. The share of people living in extreme poverty has almost halved across Asia/Pacific during the last two decades

Percentage of population living with less than USD 1.90 and USD 3.20 per day, 2000 and 2019 or nearest year available

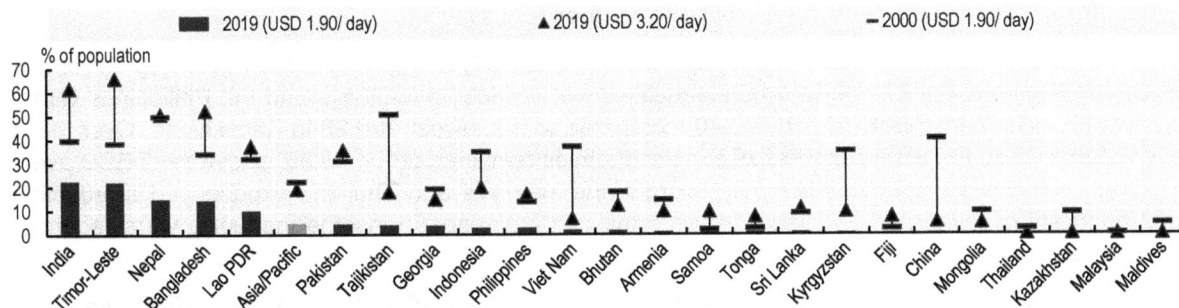

Source: World Bank (2021), World Development Indicators.

StatLink https://stat.link/qs6nv9

Figure 4.2. The death by communicable diseases is lowest in countries with a lower share of people living in extreme poverty

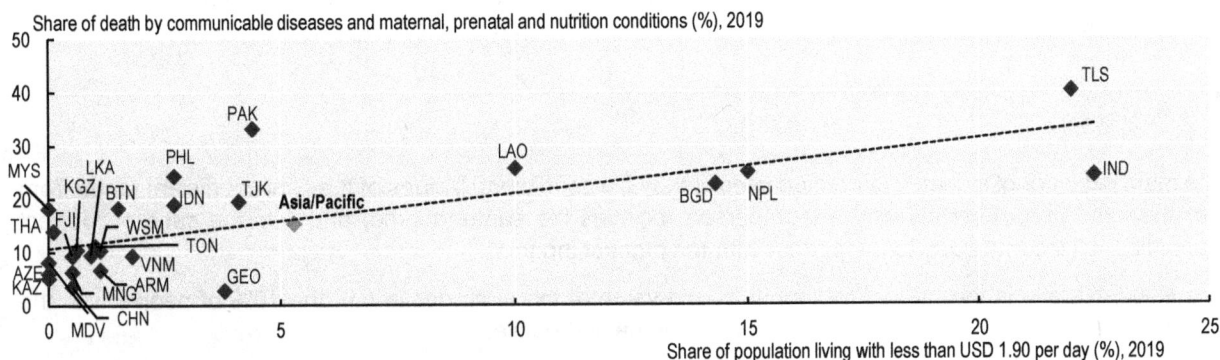

Source: World Bank (2021), World Development Indicators.

StatLink https://stat.link/h4gyns

Figure 4.3. Poverty generally declined more rapidly in countries with strong GDP growth

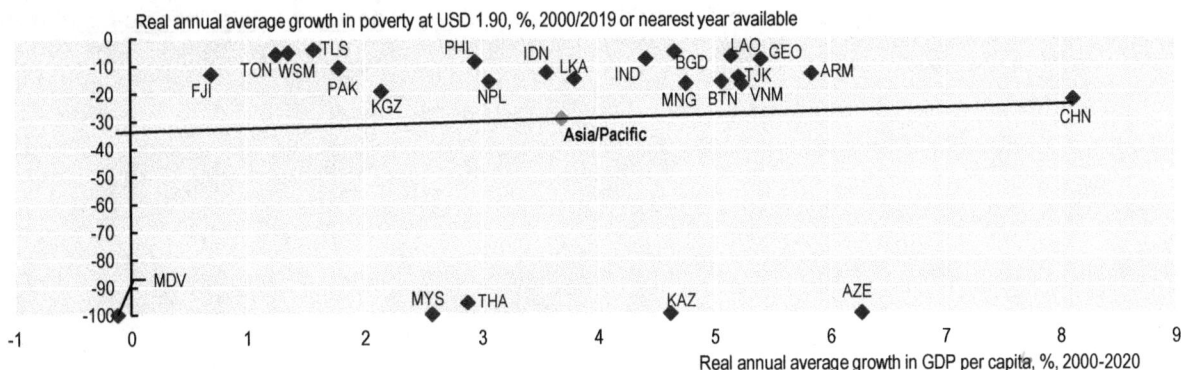

Note: Data of Real annual average growth of GDP per capita for Tonga refer to 2019.
Source: World Bank (2021), World Development Indicators.

StatLink https://stat.link/cup59f

Income inequality

Income inequality indicates how material resources are distributed across society. Some consider high levels of income inequality to be morally undesirable. Others believe that income inequality is bad because it causes conflict, limits co-operation or creates psychological and ultimately physical stresses. Often the policy concern is more for the direction of changes in inequality, rather than for its level.

Keeping measurement-related differences in mind, income inequality is high in the Asia/Pacific region compared to the OECD (Figure 4.4). In 2019, income inequalities were widest in Malaysia and the Philippines with Gini coefficients on income inequality at above 0.40, compared to the lowest at 0.28 in Kazakhstan. Over the past decade, income inequality across the Asia/Pacific economies remained around 0.35, above the OECD average (0.31). Some Asia/Pacific countries like Fiji, Georgia, the Maldives and Thailand experienced a reduction in income inequality over the past ten years, while significant increases in income inequality were recorded in Indonesia, Lao PDR and Sri Lanka.

The gap in the income distribution between the richest and the poorest 10% of the population in the Asia/Pacific economies is twice as large as in OECD countries (Figure 4.5). The gap appears widest in Malaysia and the Philippines and smallest in Kazakhstan and Timor-Leste. Over the past decade, the gap narrowed in China, Fiji, Georgia, Malaysia, the Maldives, the Philippines, and Thailand while it increased in Lao PDR, Sri Lanka and Tajikistan.

The relationship between income inequality and economic growth has stimulated much theoretical and empirical research over the past decades. However, no consensus on the strength or even the sign of the inequality-growth nexus has yet been reached. There does not appear to be a very clear country-correlation between economic growth and changes in inequalities among Asia/Pacific countries (Figure 4.6).

Definition and measurement

The main indicator of income distribution used is the Gini coefficient. Values of the Gini coefficient range from 0 in the case of "perfect equality" (each person receives the same income) and 1 in the case of "perfect inequality" (all income goes to the person with the highest income).

The P90/P10 ratio is the ratio of the upper bound value of the ninth decile (i.e. the 10% of people with the highest income) to that of the upper bound value of the first decile.

OECD measures of inequality are based on income. For Asian developing countries, where most people are self-employed in agriculture or casual labourers, income data are often not relevant or non-existent. For most countries, inequality measures are expenditure-based. Thus, country comparisons should be made with caution, as expenditure-based measures typically show lower inequality than income-based measures. Data for non-OECD Asian countries are from the World Bank Development Research Group (http://data.worldbank.org/indicator) and data for OECD countries (based on equalised disposable income) are from the OECD Income Distribution Database available at www.oecd.org/social/income-distribution-database.htm.

Figure 4.4. Income inequality across the Asia/Pacific region remains higher than in the OECD

Gini coefficient, 2009 and 2019 or latest year available

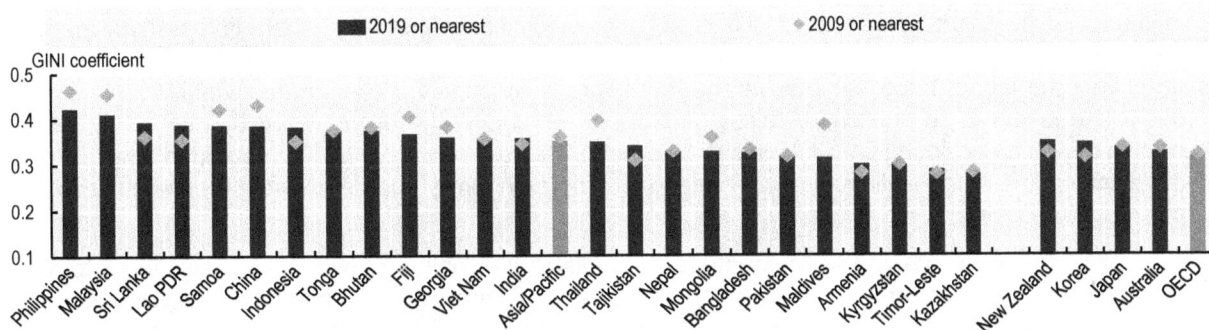

Note: The Asia/Pacific average does not include OECD four countries in this region.
Source: World Bank (2021), World Development Indicators; OECD (2021), Income Distribution Database for OECD countries.

StatLink ᵐˢᴾ https://stat.link/qusk2n

Figure 4.5. The income gap between the richest and poorest has narrowed over the past decade

Interdecile ratio P90/P10, 2010 and 2020 or latest year available

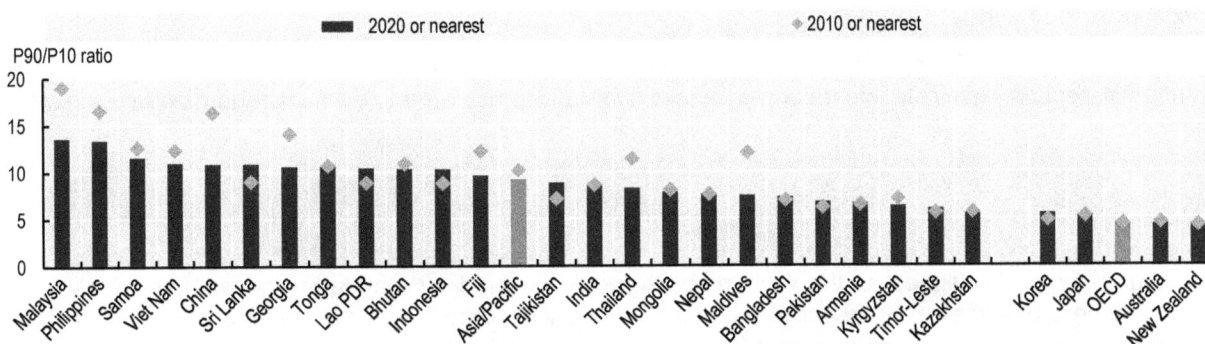

Note: The Asia/Pacific average does not include OECD countries in the region. The OECD average does not include Colombia.
Source: World Bank (2021), World Development Indicators; OECD (2021), Income Distribution Database for OECD countries.

StatLink ᵐˢᴾ https://stat.link/qrd9pu

Figure 4.6. Economic growth and income inequality seem unrelated

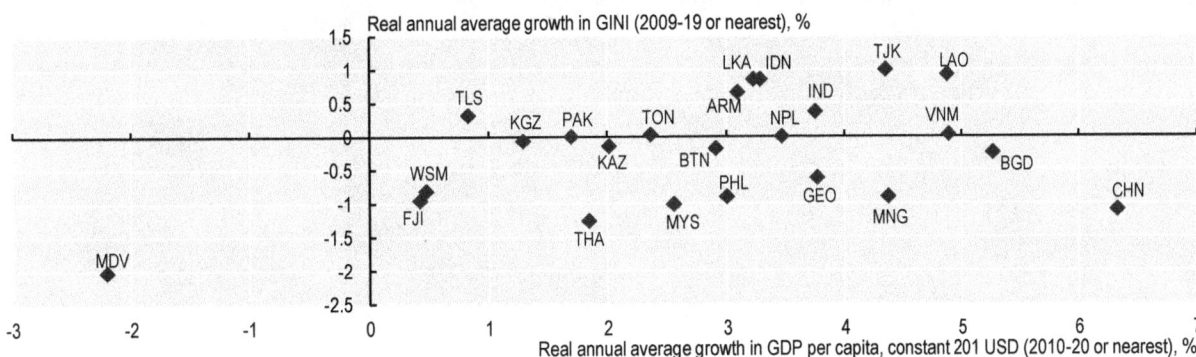

Source: World Bank (2021), World Development Indicators.

StatLink ᵐˢᴾ https://stat.link/lso6hm

Pensions: Coverage and replacement rates

The proportion of people covered by a pension scheme and the extent to which pensions replace previous earnings are two important indicators of the role pension systems play in society. There is massive variation of pension coverage in the Asia/Pacific region (Figure 4.7): in Australia, Japan and New Zealand, the pension system covers the labour force, while coverage is meagre in Indonesia, Pakistan and Viet Nam. One in two persons in the labour force and one in three persons of retirement age are covered by mandatory pension schemes in the Asia/Pacific region, while this is 87% and 97%, respectively in OECD countries. There is a risk that the elderly in the Asia/Pacific region will have to rely more on family support to meet their needs than their peers in OECD countries.

In about half of the selected Asia/Pacific countries, the redistributive nature of pension systems leads to higher replacement rates for lower earners, which is likely to have a reducing effect on income inequality among older people. However, in India, Indonesia, Pakistan, Singapore, Sri Lanka, Thailand and Viet Nam, replacement rates are the same regardless of earning levels, and thus earnings inequality is "translated" into "pension inequality".

For women, replacement rates are often below, or at best equal to, those for men without exception (Figure 4.8). In most OECD countries pensions systems as such do not lead to gender gaps in replacement rates. However, pension systems frequently generate lower replacement rates for women than for men. This is because in many countries, women have lower earnings than men, and they often retire at an earlier age and have fewer years of contributions. In addition, women have a higher life expectancy and so for countries that have DC schemes – for which sex-specific life expectancy is used, they will receive less year on year. Alongside low pension coverage, the gender pension gap will be another factor to threaten the well-being of the elderly in Asia/Pacific economies in the future.

Countries with a lower GDP per capita have lower pension coverage (Figure 4.9). In low-income countries where the informal economy prevails, most people cannot afford or do not want to participate in mandatory pension schemes.

Definition and measurement

Pension coverage is defined as the proportion of people covered by mandatory pension schemes, and measured here by i) the active labour force, and ii) recipient coverage – a ratio of persons above statutory retirement age receiving an old-age pension to all persons above statutory retirement age. The coverage value is expressed as the percentage of the population or labour force that is classified as active members of a mandatory pension system during the indicated year.

The replacement rate is often expressed as the ratio of the pension over the final earnings before retirement. However, the indicator used here shows the pension benefit as a share of individual lifetime average earnings (re-valued in line with economy-wide earnings growth). Under the baseline assumptions, workers earn the same percentage of economy-wide average earnings throughout their career. In this case, lifetime average re-valued earnings and individual final earnings are identical.

Figure 4.7. There is huge variation of pension coverage in the Asia/Pacific region

Coverage of mandatory pension systems, percentage, latest year available

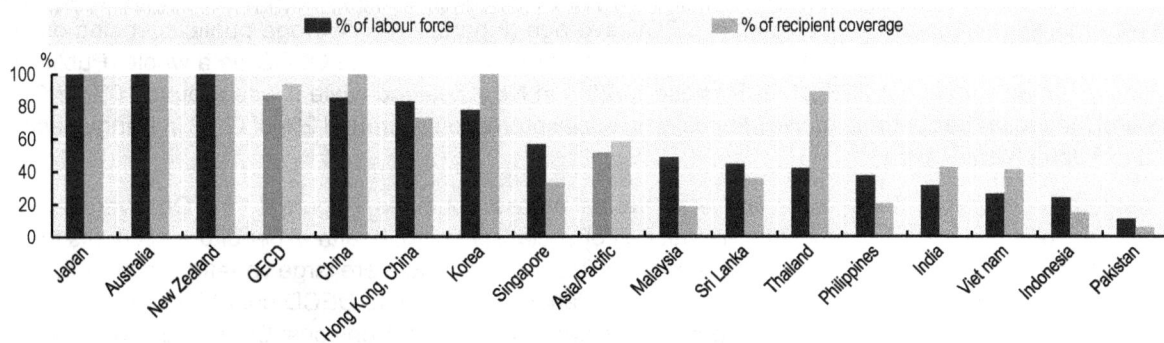

Note: Data for China, India and Indonesia refers to 2020, and data for other countries refers to 2018.
Source: World Bank (2018), pension beneficiaries' coverage; OECD (2021), *Pensions at a Glance 2021: OECD and G20 Indicators*.

StatLink https://stat.link/bjw9g5

Figure 4.8. For women replacement rates are below, or at best equal to, those for men

Gross replacement rate, mandatory pension systems, latest year available

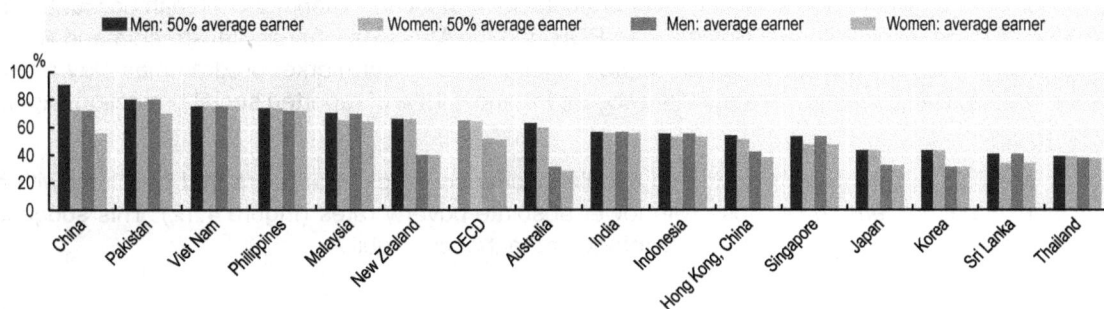

Note: Data for China, India and Indonesia refers to 2020, and data for other countries refers to 2018. OECD does not include Colombia and Lithuania.
Source: OECD (2021), *Pensions at a Glance 2021: OECD and G20 Indicators*.

StatLink https://stat.link/xdacsm

Figure 4.9. Countries with a lower GDP per capita have lower pension coverage

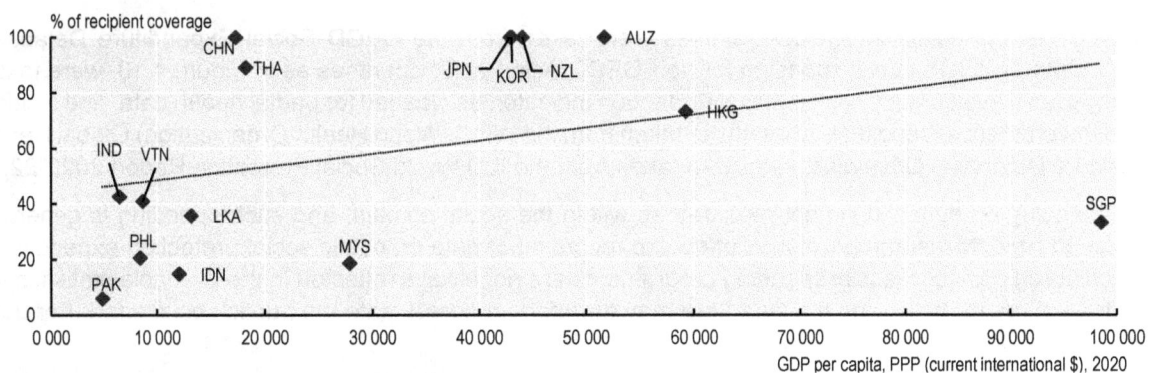

Note: Data for China, India and Indonesia refers to 2020, and data for other countries refers to 2018.
Source: World Bank (2021), World Development Indicators.

StatLink https://stat.link/0exob6

Public social expenditure

In 2018/2019, public social expenditure-to-GDP ratios varied considerably across the Asia/Pacific region. However, they were generally well below the OECD average (Figure 4.10). Average public spending on social protection in the Asia/Pacific region was about one-third of the average in the OECD as a whole. Public social spending in Japan was about 22% of GDP, close to 20% in New Zealand while it was around 10% of GDP in China and Mongolia. By contrast, public spending on social protection is around 2% of GDP in Bangladesh, Lao PDR and Papua New Guinea.

The distribution of public social spending also varies across countries (Figure 4.11). On average, public spending on social insurance accounts for almost half of social spending; health expenditure accounts for more than one-third; and, social assistance for less than one fifth. However, there are large variations across countries. Many Asia/Pacific economies have relatively young populations compared to OECD countries (see Figure 2.13), which helps to explain relatively low public spending on pension benefits (Pensions: Coverage and replacement rates).

In many Asia/Pacific countries, social insurance supports cover the relatively small public and formal sectors, and does not cover the large group of informal workers and/or self-employed workers and the elderly population who had little opportunity to contribute to pension schemes in the past. In all, social insurance benefits in many Asia/Pacific countries do not benefit the poor. Social insurance (including pensions) accounts for about 65% of reported social protection expenditure in Azerbaijan and Malaysia, whereas it is less than 5% in Georgia and the Maldives. Social assistance (including assistance for the elderly, child welfare, disability, welfare assistance) usually accounts for a relatively small share of reported social protection expenditure. Health accounts for more than two-third of social expenditure in Bhutan, Lao PDR and the Maldives whereas in Armenia and Azerbaijan only less than one fifth is dedicated to health-related risks. Active labour market programmes play a relatively small role, except in Bangladesh where ALMPs account for about 13% of reported social protection expenditure (Figure 4.11).

Considering absolute poverty rates in low- and middle-income countries, it appears that countries with higher public social expenditure tend to be those with lower absolute poverty rates (Figure 4.12). This suggests that public social spending helps to alleviate disadvantage and enhances equity.

Data and measurement

Public social expenditure concerns the provision of cash, in-kind and fiscal support to households and individuals. To be included in social spending, programmes have to involve compulsion in participation or interpersonal redistribution of resources, and address one or more contingencies, such as low income, old age, unemployment or disability. Social spending is public when general government controls the relevant financial flows.

Data on social protection for OECD countries were taken from the OECD Social Expenditure Database (SOCX). Data on public social spending for non-OECD Asia/Pacific countries as in Figure 4.10, were taken from the Asian Development Bank's Social Protection Indicator, as cleaned for partial health data, and include general government expenditure on health as taken from the WHO (World Health Organization) Global Health Expenditure Database. Otherwise, data were taken from the ILO World Social Protection Report 2020-22.

Public spending on education is not regarded as within the social domain, and such spending is generally not included here. Measurement issues affect the recording of data on public social protection expenditure; in particular regional/local social spending programmes are not always reflected in the available statistics for a country, e.g. as for India, and the data here may therefore underestimate the public social effort. For data on poverty, see the indicator Poverty.

Figure 4.10. Public social expenditure across the Asia/Pacific region is generally well below the OECD average

Public social protection expenditure as a percentage of GDP, 2018/19 or latest year available

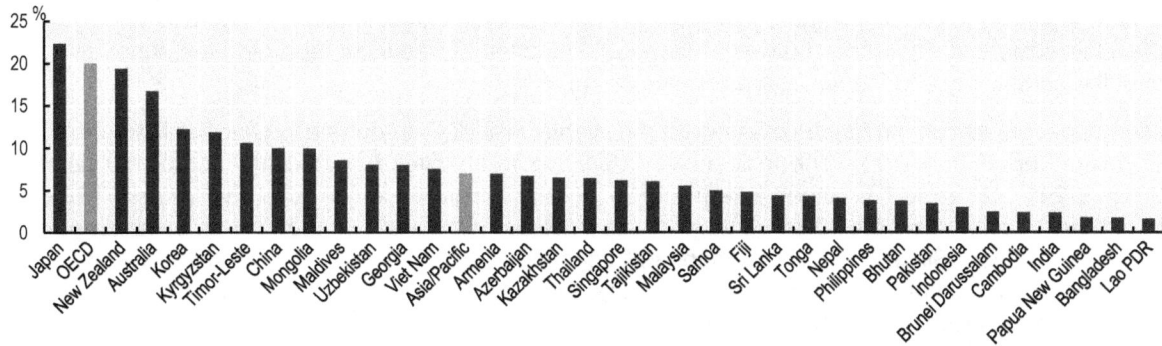

Note: Public social spending for Asia/Pacific countries non-OECD countries concerns social protection spending data from the Asian Development Bank's Social Protection Indicator, as cleaned for partial health data and also include general government expenditure on health (Government schemes and compulsory contributory health care financing schemes) as taken from the WHO (World Health Organization) Global Health Expenditure Database. Data for OECD countries refer to the OECD Social Expenditure Database (SOCX). For Brunei Darussalam, Fiji, Papua New Guinea, Samoa, Timor-Leste, and Tonga data refer to ILO World Social Protection Report 2020-22.
Source: OECD estimates based on Asian Development Bank estimates based on 2018 SPI consultants' country reports.

StatLink ᵐⁱˢᴾ https://stat.link/9k1qtw

Figure 4.11. Social spending distribution varies across countries

Public social protection expenditure by broad programme area, percentage GDP, 2018

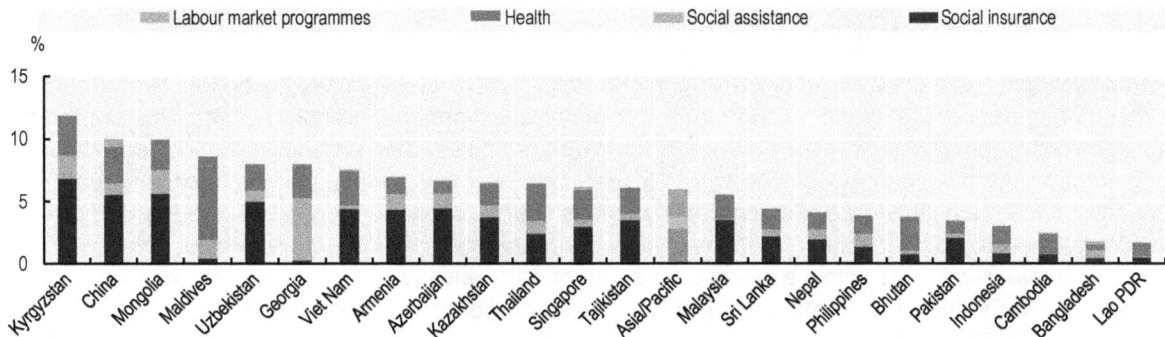

Source: OECD estimates based on Asian Development Bank estimates based on 2018 SPI consultants' country reports.

StatLink ᵐⁱˢᴾ https://stat.link/pzmu06

Figure 4.12. Public social spending and poverty

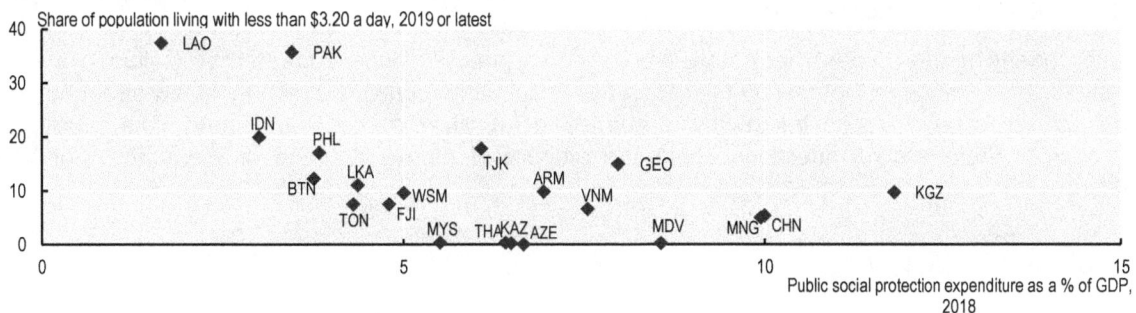

Source: OECD estimates based on Asian Development Bank estimates based on 2018 SPI consultants' country reports.

StatLink ᵐⁱˢᴾ https://stat.link/wqht6b

Solidarity

Donating to charities, doing voluntary work or helping strangers are all examples of showing compassion to others, contributing to the functioning of society and/or supporting the disadvantaged. Income levels can to some extent explain observed differences between countries, but different traditions regarding the supportive role of the state, the community and the family are also important.

On average, people across the Asia/Pacific region are slightly less likely to donate to charities than people living in OECD countries (Figure 4.13). The incidence of donating to charities has declined somewhat across the OECD since 2017/18, while it changed little in the Asia/Pacific region over the past five years (Figure 4.13). People in South-Eastern Asia are 10 percentage points more likely to donate to charity than the average across the Asia/Pacific region. Since 2010, the incidence of donating to charities has been around 15% of people in China, but this proportion had increased in recent years, most notably in 2020 – the outbreak of the COVID-19 pandemic, when the incidence exceeded 20%.

Alternative ways of showing solidarity can be through helping a stranger or offering time to an organisation or charity. In recent years, the share of people who helped a stranger increased slightly on average across the Asia/Pacific region (Figure 4.14). Indonesia and Malaysia had the largest increase in altruistic behaviour towards strangers over the past decade, while Turkmen and Bangladeshis appear to be the most likely to help a stranger in need.

The share of people who volunteered time also varies across the Asia/Pacific region (Figure 4.15). On average, one in five people volunteered time to an organisation in 2017-29. Indonesia had the highest number of volunteers, showing a large increase since 2007-09. By contrast, less than 10% of the population in Armenia, Azerbaijan, Cambodia, China and Lao PDR made time available for charitable work.

Data and measurement

Data on "solidarity" are drawn from the Gallup World Poll. The Gallup World Poll is conducted in more than 150 countries around the world based on a common questionnaire, translated into the predominant languages of each country. With few exceptions, all samples are probability-based and nationally representative of the resident population aged 15 years and over in the entire country, including rural areas. While this ensures a high degree of comparability across countries, results may be affected by sampling and non-sampling error, and variation in response rates. Hence, results should be interpreted with care. These probability surveys are valid within a statistical margin of error, also called a 95% confidence interval. This means that if the survey were conducted 100 times using the exact same procedures, the margin of error would include the "true value" in 95 out of 100 surveys. Sample sizes vary across countries from 1 000 to 4 000, and as the surveys use a clustered sample design the margin of error varies by question. The margin of error declines with increasing sample size: with a sample size of 1 000, the margin of error at a 95% confidence interval is $0.98/\sqrt{}$ (sample size) or 3%; with a sample size of 4 000, this is 1.5%. To minimise the effect of annual fluctuations in responses related to small sample sizes, results are averaged over a three-year period, or two-year period in case of missing data. If only one observation in a three-year period is available, this finding is not reported.

The data underlying the solidarity indicators are based on binary questions created by Gallup: "Have you done any of the following in the past month? How about donating money to a charity? How about helped a stranger or someone you didn't know who needed help? How about volunteering your time to an organisation?" There are no questions about the amount of money donated or the number of hours volunteered.

Figure 4.13. The propensity to give to charity varies widely across Asia/Pacific countries

Share of people who have donated money to a charity from 2010 to 2020, in selected country and areas

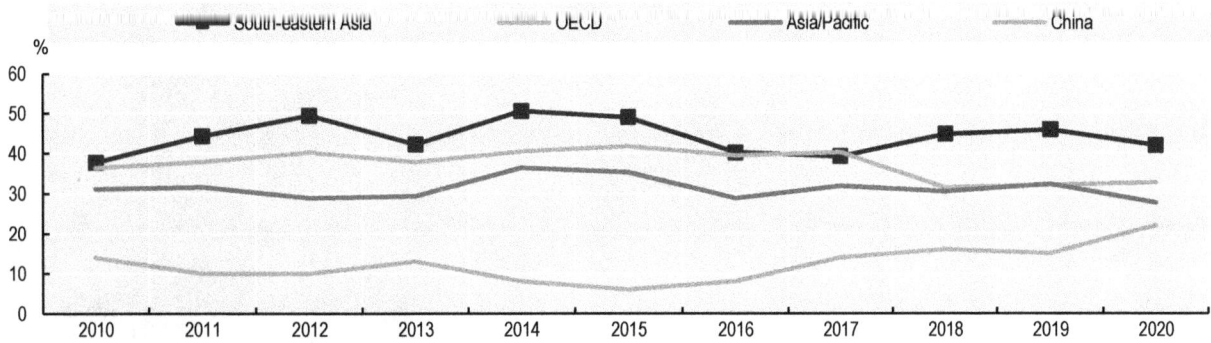

Source: Gallup World Poll (2021), www.gallup.com.

StatLink ᴹˢᴾ https://stat.link/evhqit

Figure 4.14. The share of people who helped a stranger increased slightly across Asia/Pacific

Share of people who helped a stranger or someone they didn't know who needed help in the past month (%)

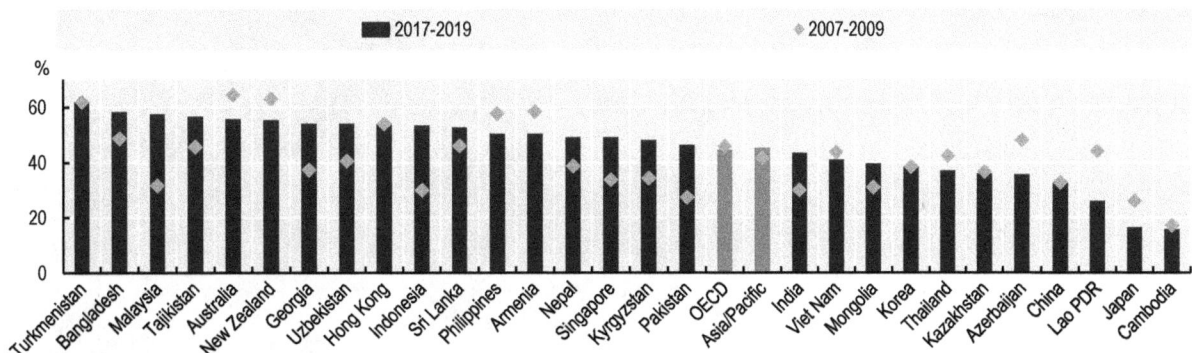

Source: Gallup World Poll (2021), www.gallup.com.

StatLink ᴹˢᴾ https://stat.link/xh3l6k

Figure 4.15. On average, one in four people volunteers time to a charitable organisation across Asia/Pacific and the OECD

Share of people who volunteered time to an organisation in the past month (%)

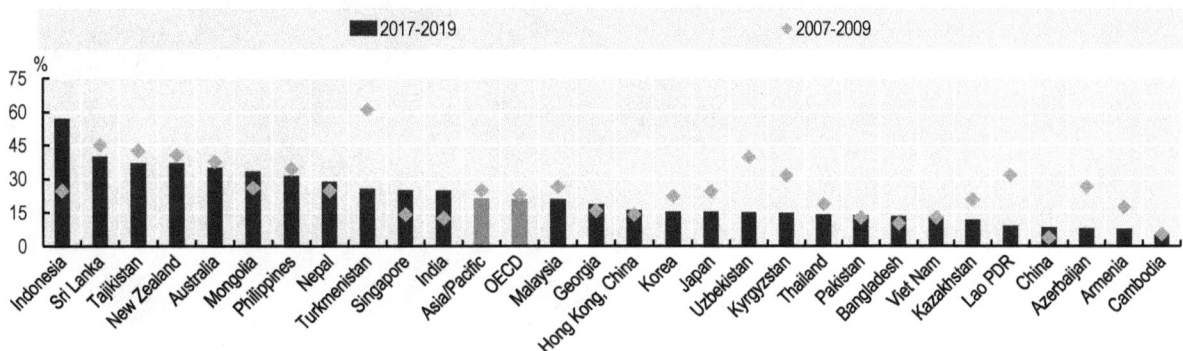

Source: Gallup World Poll (2021), www.gallup.com.

StatLink ᴹˢᴾ https://stat.link/hr4mbn

5 Health

Life expectancy

Life expectancy at birth is a general measure of a population's health status, and is often used to gauge the development of a country's health. Life expectancy at birth continues to rise in Asia and the Pacific, averaging about 74.2 years in 2019 up from 68.6 years in 2000 (Figure 5.1). Since 2000, the largest increases in life expectancy were recorded for Cambodia (11.4 years), Bhutan (10.9 years) and Timor-Leste (10.5 years). This rapid growth is related to a number of factors, including rising living standards, better nutrition, water and sanitation, increased education and greater access to health services. Nevertheless, despite the significant increase, life expectancy in the Asia/Pacific still lags behind other world regions except Sub-Saharan Africa (United Nations, 2019[1]).

There is large cross-national variation in life expectancy across the region: life expectancy at birth is 80 years or more in East Asia, while this is 70 years or less in some Southern and South-Eastern Asian countries (Cambodia, Lao PDR, Pakistan and Turkmenistan) as well as the island nations of Papua New Guinea and Fiji. On average in the Asia/Pacific region women outlive men by almost five years. Women in Georgia and Kazakhstan outlive men by 8.5 years or more, while this less than one year in Bhutan. Women in Hong Kong, China have the highest life expectancy at birth at over 88 years compared to 82 years for men.

More and more people in Asia become senior citizens. About 90% of population reach the age of 65 in Australia, Japan, Hong Kong, China, Korea, Macau, China, the Maldives, New Zealand and Singapore (Figure 5.2). Men in Fiji, Mongolia and Turkmenistan and men and women in Papua New Guinea are least likely to celebrate their own 65th birthday – less than 70% for women and 65% for men.

Higher national income, measured by GDP per capita, is generally associated with longer life expectancy at birth (Figure 5.3). However, the linkages between income and life expectancy are not always that strong. For example, Viet Nam has one of the lowest incomes per capita in the region at about USD 8 650, but has a relatively high life expectancy at 75 years on average. In comparison, Brunei Darussalam has a similar life expectancy at 76 years on average, but its GDP per capita of USD 65 660 is seven times as high as in Viet Nam.

Definition and measurement

Life expectancy measures how long, on average, a new-born infant would live if the prevailing patterns of mortality at the time of birth were to stay the same throughout their lifetime. Since the factors that affect life expectancy do not change overnight, variations are best assessed over long periods of time. Countries calculate life expectancy according to methodologies that can vary somewhat, and these can lead to differences of fractions of a year. Some countries base their life expectancies on estimates derived from censuses and surveys, and not on the accurate registration of deaths.

Survival rate to age 65 refers to the percentage of a cohort of new-born infants that would survive to age 65, if subject to current age-specific mortality rates.

The economy-wide (GDP) Purchasing Power Parities (PPPs) are used as they are readily available conversion rates. These are based on a broad basket of goods and services, chosen to be representative of all economic activity. The use of economy-wide PPPs means that the resulting variations in health expenditure across countries might reflect not only variations in the volume of health services, but also any variations in the prices of health services relative to prices in the rest of the economy.

Reference

United Nations (2019), *UN World Population Prospects 2019*, https://population.un.org/wpp/.   [1]

Figure 5.1. Life expectancy at birth continues to rise in the Asia/Pacific region

Life expectancy at birth, by sex, 2000 and 2019

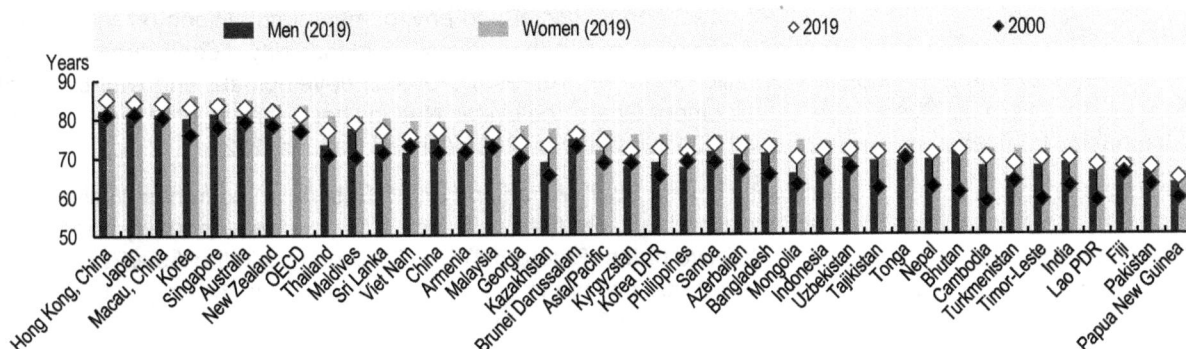

Source: OECD (2021), OECD Health Statistics; for other countries, World Bank (2021), World Development Indicators.

StatLink https://stat.link/ha7db4

Figure 5.2. More and more people, in Asia reach the age of 65

Survival rate to age 65 (% of cohort), by sex, 2000 and 2019

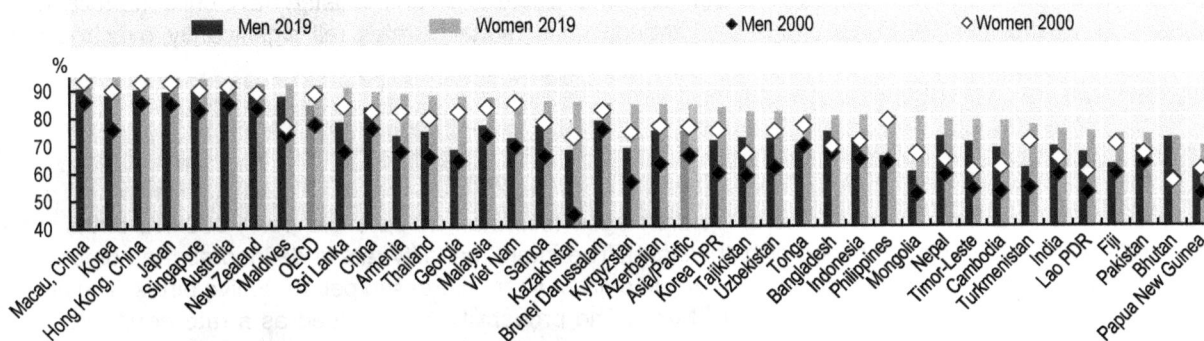

Source: World Bank (2021), World Development Indicators.

StatLink https://stat.link/l87smf

Figure 5.3. Higher national income (as measured by GDP per capita) is generally associated with higher life expectancy at birth

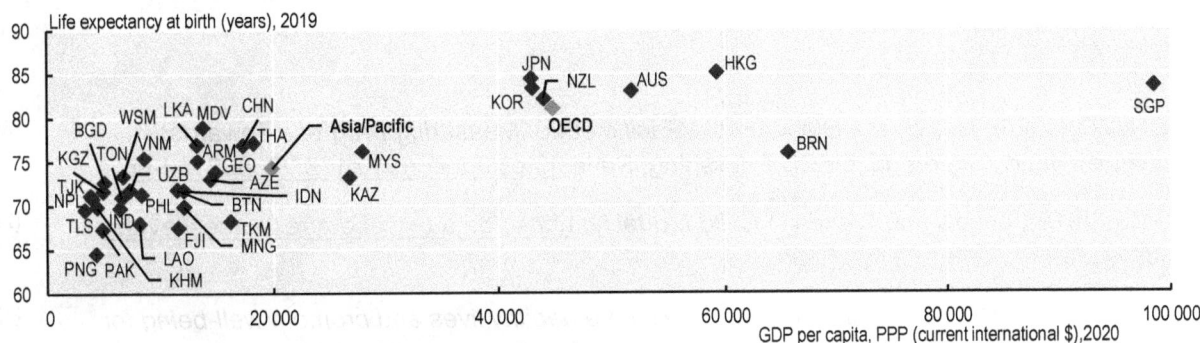

Source: OECD (2021), OECD National Accounts; OECD (2021), OECD Health Statistics; for other countries, World Bank (2021), World Development Indicators.

StatLink https://stat.link/9y6squ

Neonatal, infant and child mortality

Neonatal mortality – death among children less than 28 days, as well as infant mortality – death among children not yet one year of age, reflect the effect of economic, social and environmental conditions on the health of mothers and new-borns, as well as the effectiveness of health systems. Child mortality – death among children not yet 5 years of age is an indicator of child health as well as the overall development and well-being of a population. As part of the Sustainable Development Goals, the United Nations has set a target of reducing under age 5 mortality to at least as low as 25 per 1 000 live births by 2030 (United Nations, 2021[1]).

The neonatal mortality rates are persistently high in South Asian and South East Asian countries. While rates in Bangladesh, Cambodia, India and Nepal declined by more than half since 2000, neonatal mortality rates remain high in Pakistan at over 40 deaths per 1 000 live births (Figure 5.4). OECD countries in the Asia/Pacific region have neonatal mortality rates of 3 deaths per 1 000 live births or less, but Singapore is the only country where the neonatal mortality rate was below 1 death per 1 000 live births in 2019.

Across the selected countries, the highest incidence of infant mortality is recorded for children with mothers with low educational attainment and little income (Figure 5.5). While all the selected countries show similar trends, the infant mortality differences related to socio-economic status of mothers were widest in Lao PDR (2017): the infant mortality rate was 56 among low-income families and 19 for high-income families; 49 for mothers with low educational attainment and 7 for mothers with high educational attainment.

Child mortality rates have halved over the 2000-19 period. However, one-third of Asia/Pacific countries have not yet achieved the Sustainable Development Goal of a child mortality rate of 25 or less per 1 000 live births (Figure 5.6). Lao PDR, Pakistan, Papua New Guinea, Timor-Leste and Turkmenistan have child mortality rates exceeding 40 deaths per 1 000 live births even though child mortality rates fell significantly over the past 15 years.

Definition and measurement

Neonatal mortality is defined as deaths of children aged less than 28 days old per 1 000 live births (no minimum threshold of gestation period or birthweight). The infant mortality rate is defined as the number of children who die before reaching their first birthday in a given year, expressed per 1 000 live births. The child mortality rate (or under-five mortality rate – U5MR) is the probability – expressed as a rate per 1 000 live births, of a child born in a specified years dying before reaching the age of five when subject to current age-specific mortality rates.

Some countries base their infant mortality rates on estimates derived from censuses, surveys and sample registration systems, and not on accurate and complete registration of births and deaths. Differences among countries in registering practices for premature infants may also add to international variations in rates.

References

OECD/WHO (2020), *Health at a Glance: Asia/Pacific 2020: Measuring Progress Towards Universal Health Coverage*, OECD Publishing, Paris, https://doi.org/10.1787/26b007cd-en. [3]

UN IGME (2019), *Levels and Trends in Child Mortality*, https://data.unicef.org/resources/levels-and-trends-in-child-mortality-2019/. [2]

United Nations (2021), *SDG Indicators-Goal 3. Ensure healthy lives and promote well-being for all at all ages*, https://unstats.un.org/sdgs/metadata/files/Metadata-03-02-01.pdf. [1]

Figure 5.4. The neonatal mortality rate has halved, while huge disparities exist across countries

Neonatal mortality rate, per 1 000 live births, 2000 and 2019

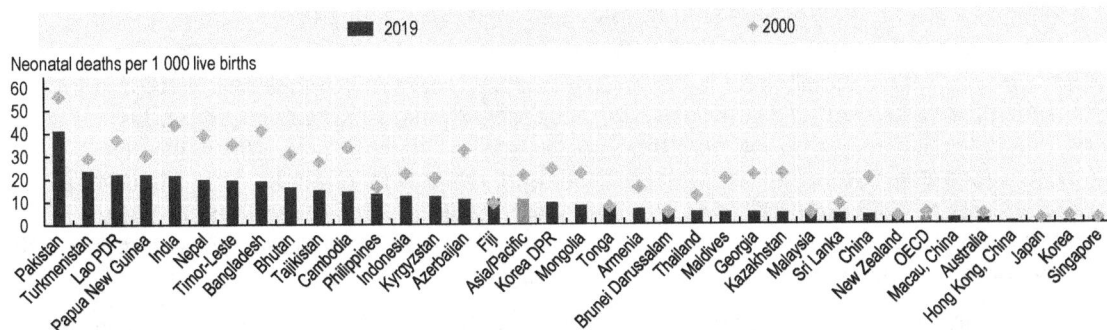

Source: UN Inter-Agencies Group for Child Mortality Estimation (UN IGME) (2021), Neonatal mortality rate; Hong Kong annual digest of statistics (2019); Macau yearbook of Statistics (2020).

StatLink https://stat.link/orjub6

Figure 5.5. Mothers experienced high incidence of infant mortality when they have low education and wealth

Infant mortality rate by wealth and mothers' education, selected countries and years

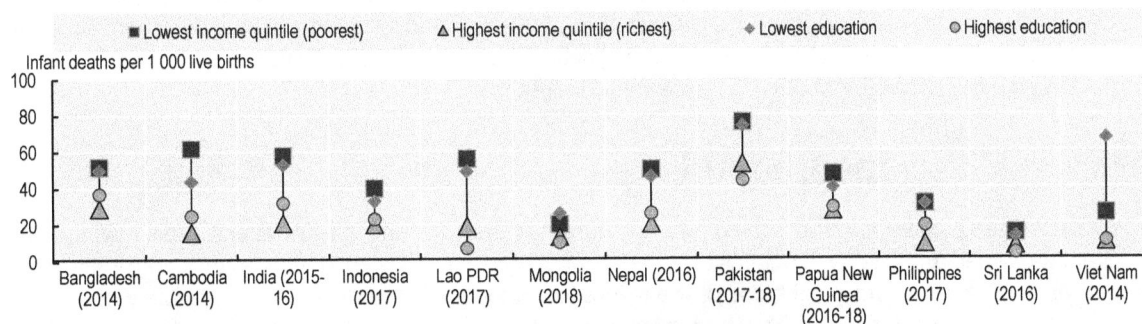

Note: Income quintiles data for Viet Nam refer to the 40% poorest and the 60% richest population.
Source: OECD/WHO (2020), Health at a Glance: Asia/Pacific 2020: Measuring Progress Towards Universal Health Coverage.

StatLink https://stat.link/57g10s

Figure 5.6. The child mortality rate decreased more than half since 2000

Child (under 5) mortality, per 1 000 live births, by sex, 2000 and 2019

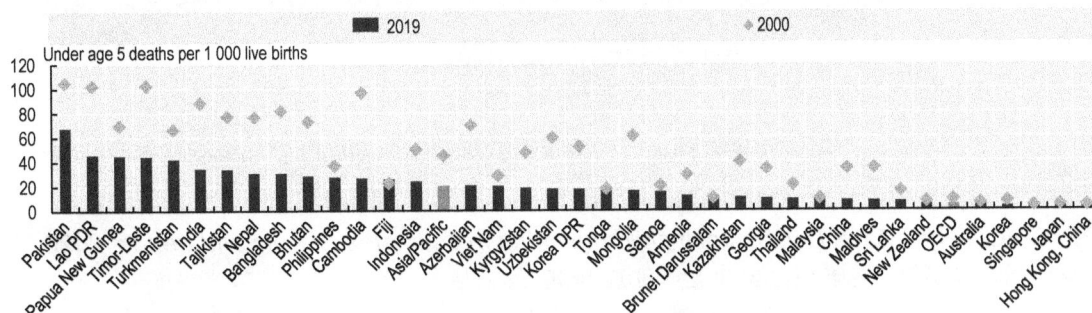

Note: Data for Hong Kong, China refers to 2018.
Source: UN IGME (2021); Social Indicators of Hong Kong (2018), under age 5 child mortality per 1 000 live births.

StatLink https://stat.link/kwuo8v

Child malnutrition (including under nutrition and overweight)

National development is largely dependent on healthy and well-nourished people. However, there are many children who are not always able to access sufficient, safe, nutritious food and a balanced diet that meet their needs for optimal growth and development. Poor nutrition in utero and early childhood often results in stunting which refers to a child who is too short for his or her age. Similarly wasting, a child who is too thin for his or her height, is usually the result form a poor diet and/or disease. Stunting and wasting often lead to noticeable educational and economic disadvantages that could last a lifetime and affect the next generation (UNICEF;WHO;World Bank Group, 2018[1]). On the other end, overweight or obese children, too heavy for their height, are at greater risk of poor health and reduced quality of life in adolescence and in adulthood. The UN SDG target 2.2 involves "ending all forms of malnutrition by 2030, including achieving, by 2025, the internationally agreed targets on stunting and wasting in children under 5 years of age".

Many countries in the Asia/Pacific region have a high prevalence of stunting and wasting among children. Fortunately, however, over the 2000-19 period the prevalence of stunting (low height-for-age) and wasting (low weight-for-height) among children not yet 5 years of age diminished from 30 to 20% and from 9 to 6% respectively (Figure 5.7). Stunting prevalence is highest at around 50% in Papua New Guinea and Timor-Leste, while it is below 3% in Australia, Korea and Tonga. The prevalence of wasting is highest in India, Nepal, Papua New Guinea, and Sri Lanka. Over the past 19 years, the prevalence of wasting among children under 5 increased most in Indonesia (5 percentage points) and Bhutan (3 percentage points). Countries with a higher prevalence of underweight children have higher child mortality rates (Figure 5.8): nearly half of the deaths among children under age 5 are related to undernutrition (UN IGME, 2019[2]).

The prevalence of children under 5 who are overweight varies: it is above 20% in Australia, while it is negligible in India, Japan and Timor-Leste (Figure 5.9). Over the 2000-19 period, the proportion of children under 5 overweight increased by more than 10 percentage points in Australia and Papua New Guinea, while the Asia/Pacific average increased by about 1.5 percentage points.

Definition and measurement

The WHO definition of child stunting is height-for-age greater than 2 standard deviations below WHO Child Growth Standards median. The WHO definition of child wasting refers to a child who is too thin for his or her height as a result of recent rapid weight loss or the failure to gain weight. A child who is moderately or severely wasted has an increased risk of death, but treatment is possible. The prevalence of child wasting refers to the percentage of children under age 5 whose weight for height is greater than 2 standard deviations below WHO Child Growth Standards median. The WHO definition of prevalence of underweight is the percentage of children under age 5 whose weight-for-age-ratio is more than 2 standard deviations below the World Health Organization (WHO) Child Growth Standards median. The WHO definition of children overweight is weight-for-height greater than 2 standard deviations above WHO Child Growth Standards median. The WHO definition of child obesity is weight-for-height greater than 3 standard deviations above the WHO Child Growth Standards median.

References

UN IGME (2019), *Levels and Trends in Child Mortality*, https://data.unicef.org/resources/levels-and-trends-in-child-mortality-2019/.   [2]

UNICEF; WHO; World Bank (2020), *Joint child malnutrition estimates: Levels and trends: 2020 edition*, https://data.unicef.org/resources/jme-report-2020/.   [3]

UNICEF;WHO;World Bank Group (2018), *Levels and trends in child malnutrition, Joint Child Malnutrition Estimates, Key findings of the 2018 edition*.   [1]

Figure 5.7. Many countries in the Asia/Pacific region have a high prevalence of stunting and wasting among young children

Prevalence among children under 5 (%), 2000 and 2019 latest year available

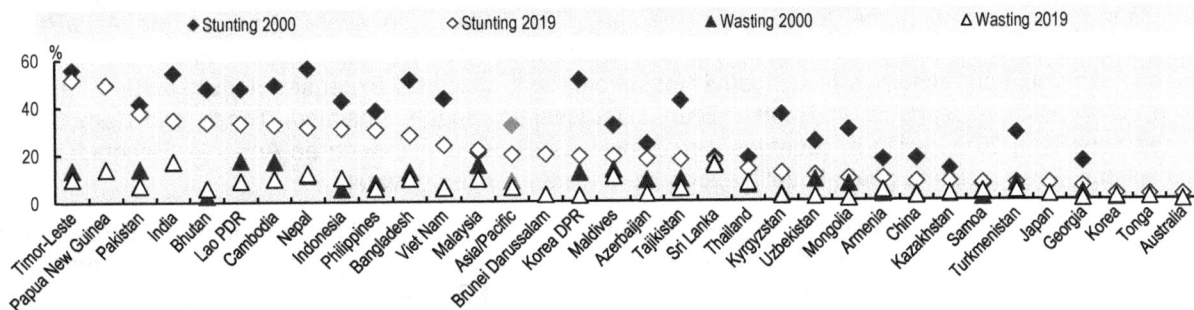

Source: UNICEF/WHO/World Bank (2021), Joint Child Malnutrition Estimates Expanded Database, October 2021, Paris

StatLink https://stat.link/sqkl4w

Figure 5.8. Countries with a higher prevalence of underweight children have higher child mortality rates

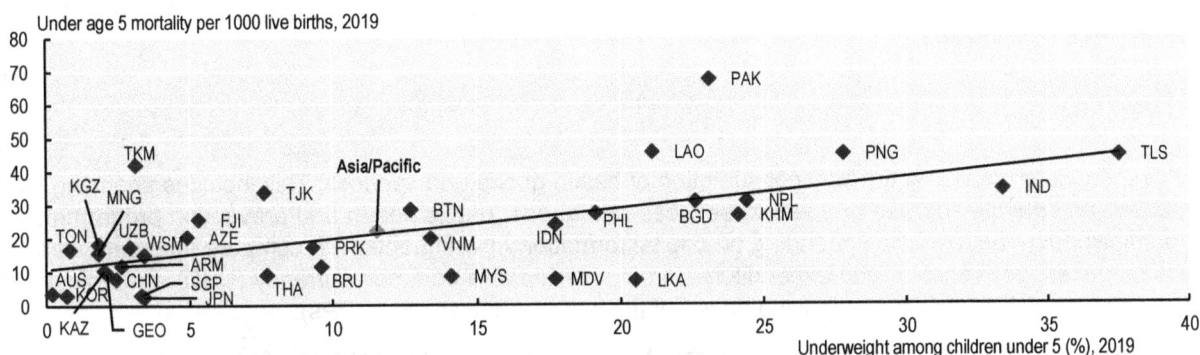

Source: UNICEF/WHO/World Bank (2021), Joint Child Malnutrition Estimates Expanded Database, October 2021, Paris. For child mortality rate: UN IGME (2021); Social Indicators of Hong Kong (2018), under age 5 child mortality per 1 000 live births.

StatLink https://stat.link/dsqgf8

Figure 5.9. The number of overweight children has increased in most Asia/Pacific countries

Prevalence of overweight among children under 5 (%), 2000 and 2019 or latest year available

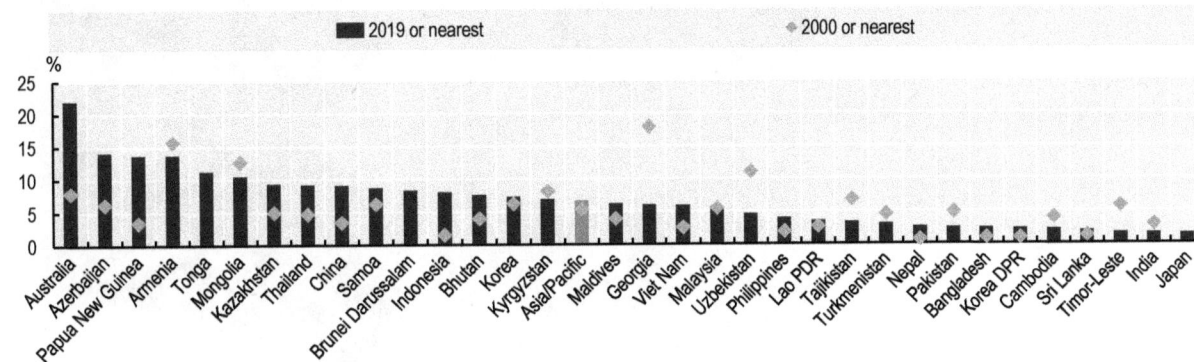

Source: UNICEF/WHO/World Bank (2021), Joint Child Malnutrition Estimates Expanded Database, October 2021, Paris.

StatLink https://stat.link/dwme4z

Health expenditure

Financial resources for health are unevenly distributed geographically. Australia, Japan and Singapore have higher health expenditure per capita than the OECD average (USD 4 100, 2018), while most of Asia/Pacific economies spend less than the Asia/Pacific average (USD 1 090). On average across the Asia/Pacific, two-thirds of health expenditure is financed by governments or compulsory insurance schemes, and the rest is financed from voluntary schemes or concerns households' out-of-pocket expenses (Figure 5.10). More than 80% of total health expenditure in Bhutan, Brunei Darussalam, Japan, Thailand, Tonga and Samoa were financed publicly in 2018, while in countries with a lower GDP per capita such as Armenia, Bangladesh and Turkmenistan, three-quarters of total health expenditure were financed privately.

On average the Asia/Pacific economies experienced annual growth in real health expenditure in GDP per capita of 6.4% over the 2010-18 period (Figure 5.11). Spending on health expenditure per capita in China, Timor-Leste and Turkmenistan grew rapidly in comparison to the growth-rate of GDP per capita. In contrast, in Fiji, Georgia and Lao PDR health expenditure increased by less than what might have been expected on basis of the annual increase in GDP per capita.

Health expenditure as a percentage of GDP grew steadily in most Asia/Pacific countries over the past decade (Figure 5.12). However, compared with the OECD average (8.7%), average health expenditure in the Asia/Pacific region remains relatively low (5.2%). There is also considerable variation across the region: health expenditure in some South East Asian countries such as Bangladesh, Brunei Darussalam, Indonesia, Kazakhstan, Lao PDR and Papua New Guinea was less than 3% of GDP in 2018, while it was in excess of 10% of GDP in Armenia and Japan.

Definition and measurement

Heath expenditure measures the final consumption of health goods and services. This includes spending by both public and private sources on medical services and goods, public health and prevention programmes and administration, but excludes spending on capital formation (investments). To compare spending levels across countries, per capita health expenditures are converted to a common currency (USD) and adjusted to take account of the different purchasing power of the national currencies (PPPs).

The financing of health care can be analysed from the point of view of the sources of funding (households, employers and the state), financing schemes (compulsory or voluntary insurance), and financing agents (organisations managing the financing schemes). Here "financing" is used in the sense of financing schemes as defined in the System of Health Accounts (OECD/WHO/Eurostat, 2011). Public financing includes expenditure by the general government and social security funds. Private financing covers households' out-of-pocket payments, private health insurance and other private funds (NGOs and private corporations).

Figure 5.10. Total health expenditure varies considerably across the Asia/Pacific region

Total health expenditure per capita, public and private, USD PPP, 2018

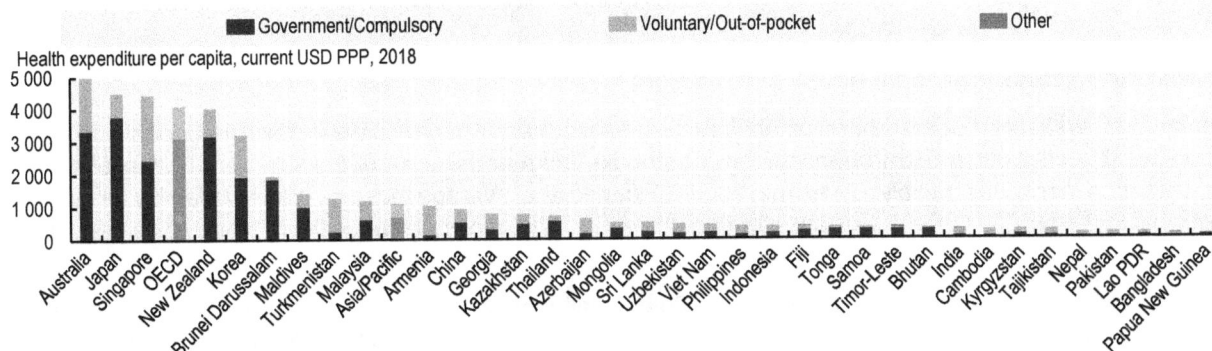

Note: Other refers to unspecified financing schemes (n.e.c.).
Source: WHO (2021), Global Health Expenditure Database.

StatLink https://stat.link/zsh2ey

Figure 5.11. Trends in health expenditure and GDP per capita vary across countries

Average annual growth of health expenditure and GDP per capita 2010-18

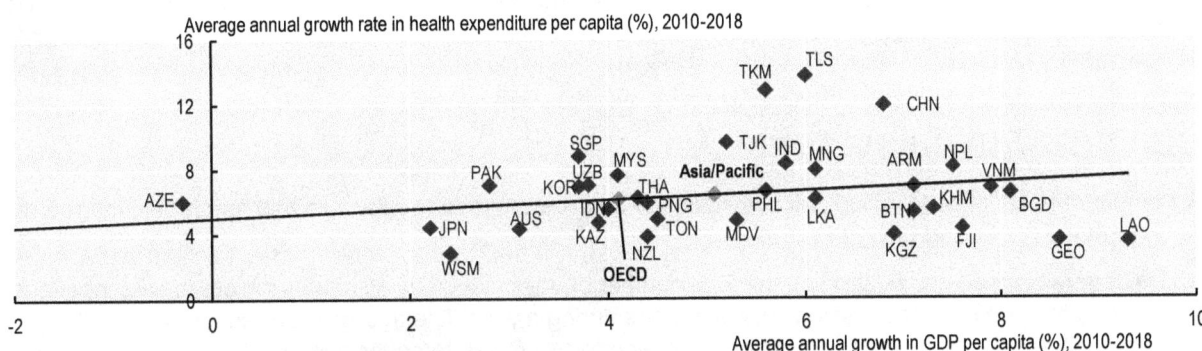

Source: WHO (2021), Global Health Expenditure Database.

StatLink https://stat.link/4khqy3

Figure 5.12. Health expenditure-to-GDP-ratios increased in many Asian/Pacific countries

Current health expenditure (%) of Gross domestic product (GDP) in 2010 and 2018

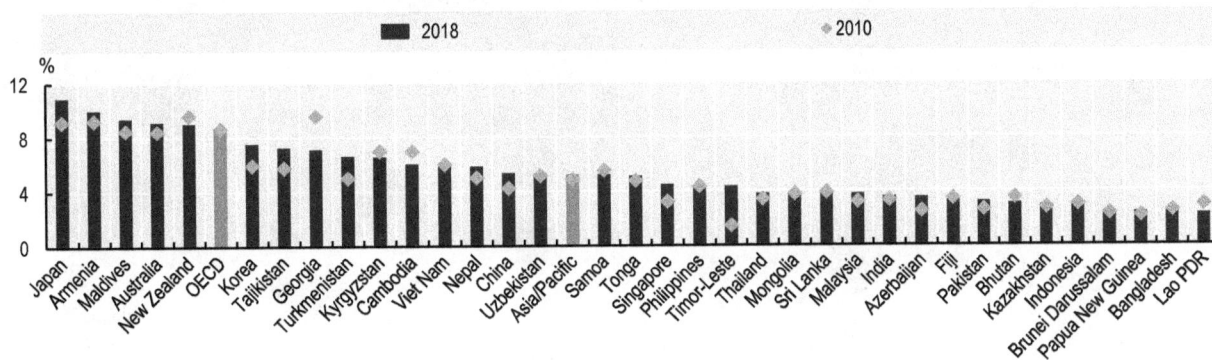

Source: WHO (2021), Global Health Expenditure Database; OECD (2021), OECD Health Statistics.

StatLink https://stat.link/p7o4yb

Hospital activities

Hospitals in most countries account for the largest part of overall fixed health investment. It is important to use resources efficiently and assure co-ordinated access to hospital care: the number of hospital beds, hospital discharge rates and the average length of stay (ALOS) are among the indicators used to assess available resources and access in general.

Hospital bed availability varies considerably across the Asia/Pacific region. It is highest in Japan and Korea (Figure 5.13). At the other end, in Bangladesh, Cambodia, India and Pakistan, the number of hospital-beds is less than one per 1 000 people. Over the 2005-20 period the average hospital bed availability diminished somewhat in the OECD. In the Asia/Pacific region, the availability of hospital beds fell in Nepal, but increased in China and Korea.

The hospital discharge rate is at 130 cases per 1 000 population on average in Asia/Pacific countries, compared with the OECD average of 151 (Figure 5.14, Panel A). The highest hospital discharge rates were recorded for Sri Lanka and Mongolia, with over 300 and 250 discharges per 1 000 population in a year respectively. By contrast, in Bangladesh, discharge rates were below 25 cases per 1 000 population. Increasing the number of beds and overnight stays in hospitals does not always bring positive outcomes in population health. Hence, ALOS is also used to assess appropriate access and use. In the Asia/Pacific region, the average length of stay (ALOS) for acute care is 5.7 days on average, slightly below the OECD average of 7.7 days (Figure 5.14, Panel B). The longest ALOS is 16 days in Japan, while the shortest is 2.5 days in Lao PDR and Bangladesh.

In general, countries with more hospital beds tend to have higher discharge rates as well as longer ALOS (Figure 5.15). However, there are some exceptions: Japan and Korea, with the highest number of hospital beds per population, have a relatively low discharge rate while Sri Lanka, with average bed availability, has the highest discharge rate.

Definition and measurement

The number of hospital beds include all hospital beds such as those for acute care and for chronic/long-term care, in both the public and private sectors.

ALOS is generally measured by dividing the total number of days stayed by all patients in acute care inpatient institutions by the number of admissions or discharges during a year. The figures reported for average length of stay (ALOS) are for acute care only. In general reported ALOS data cover only public sector institutions, and only a few countries, such as China, Mongolia and Thailand, comprehensively cover private sector institutions in their ALOS statistics.

A discharge is defined as the release of a patient who has stayed at least one night in hospital, and it includes deaths in hospital following inpatient care. The discharge rates presented here are not age-standardised, i.e. they do not take account for cross-national differences in the age structure of populations. The figures presented here come mostly from administrative sources.

Figure 5.13. The average hospital bed availability varies widely across the Asia/Pacific region

Hospital beds per 1 000 population, 2005 and 2020 or latest year available

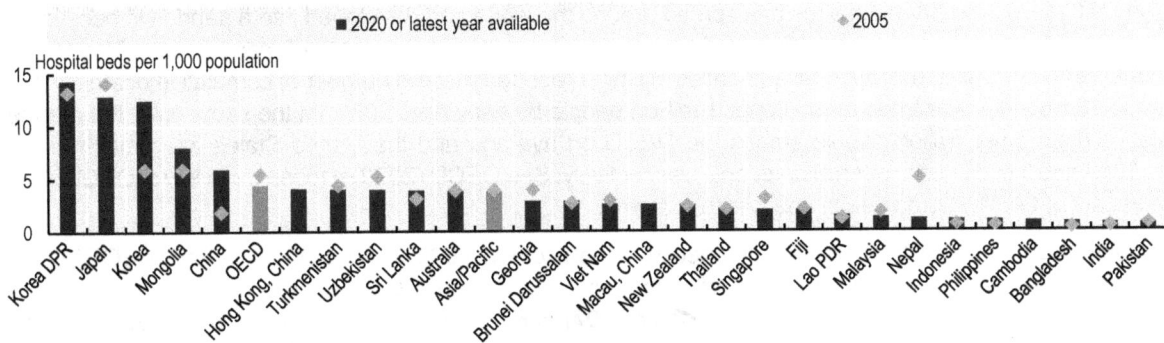

Source: OECD (2021) OECD Health Statistics; WHO (2020)Global Health Observatory; Hong Kong annual statistic digest (2019), National sources.

StatLink https://stat.link/65twrp

Figure 5.14. Hospital discharge rates and ALOS vary widely across countries

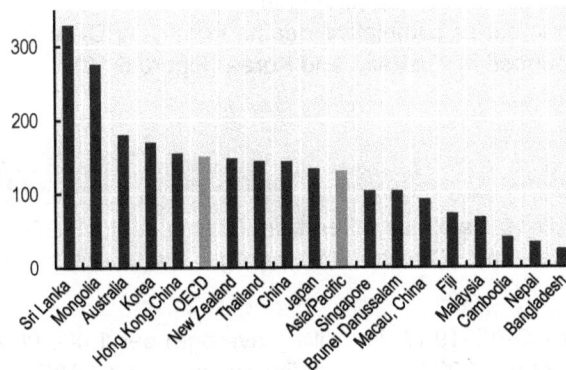 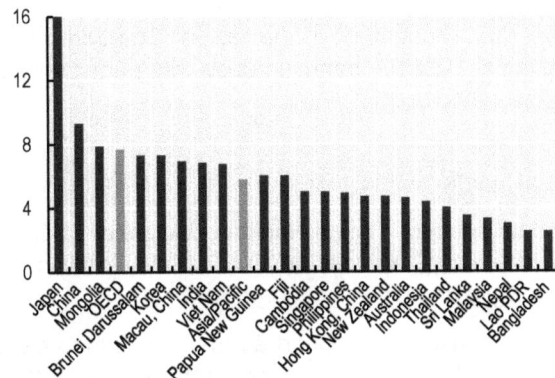

Source: OECD (2021), Hospital discharge rates (indicator); OECD (2021), Length of hospital stay (indicator); WHO Global Health Observatory data 2018.

StatLink https://stat.link/3zhi48

Figure 5.15. Countries with more hospital beds tend to have higher discharge rates and longer ALOS

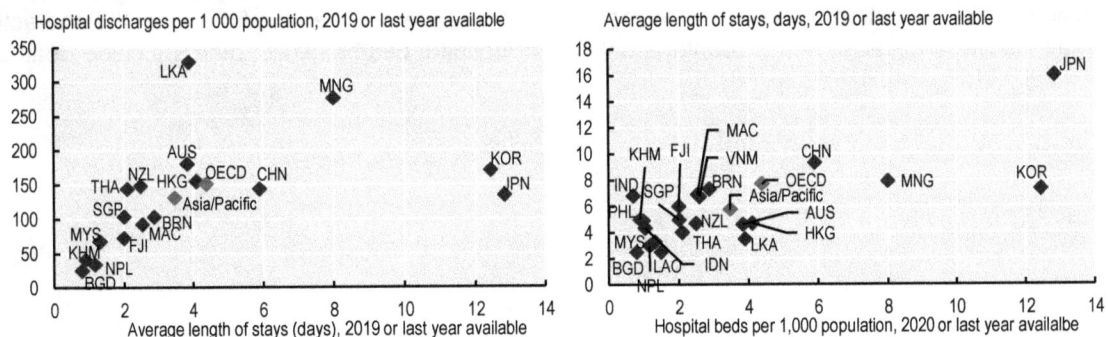

Source: OECD (2021) OECD Health Statistics; WHO (2020), Global Health Observatory; Hong Kong Annual Digest of Statistics (2019), National sources.

StatLink https://stat.link/fat05h

COVID-19

The first COVID-19 cases were confirmed in Wuhan, China, in late 2019 (Huang et al., 2020[1]; Roberts, Rossman and Jarić, 2021[2]). Since then the virus has spread around the world and developed into a pandemic because of its contagious characteristics and the associated illnesses, which resulted in the death of many people. The pandemic may have started in China, but, national authorities in China reported that the number of cumulative deaths attributed to COVID-19 was just over three persons per 1 million people by early April 2022. At the same time, the number of cumulative deaths per million people across the OECD on average and the United States were much higher at almost 2000 and 3 000 deaths per million people, respectively. See OECD (2022[3]) for an overview of OECD analysis on the impact of COVID-19 on health and health systems.

The number of new COVID-19 cases remained relatively low in 2020 in Asia and the Pacific (OECD/WHO, 2020[4]). By the end of 2020, the number of cumulative deaths from COVID-19 per 1 million persons was relatively low in China (3), Indonesia (81) and India (107) compared to the OECD average (620) while in the United States already over 1 000 persons per 1 million people had died from COVID-19 (Ritchie et al., 2022[5]). However, in mid-2021 the number of new cases spiked in India, Indonesia and Japan (Figure 5.16), contributing to a significant increase in the number of cumulative deaths in these countries in 2021(Figure 5.18).

The emergence of the "Omicron variant" – highly contagious (the scales of the number of cases as reported in Figure 5.16 and Figure 5.17 are very different), contributed to the rapid increase in the number of cases in Australia around Christmas 2021 peaking in January 2022. "Omicron" also contributed to the case numbers reaching new heights in New Zealand and Korea in early and late March 2022, respectively (Figure 5.17). By comparison, the increase in case numbers in India, Indonesia in the first quarter of 2022 was limited. Indeed, the number of cumulative deaths in India and Indonesia changed little in the first quarter of 2022, in contrast to the four OECD countries in the region. Compared to the number of cumulative deaths from COVID-19 at the beginning of 2022 the trend increase was particularly pronounced in Australia and Korea (Figure 5.18).

Definition and measurement

The data concern "Johns Hopkins University CSSE COVID-19 Data", as taken from Ritchie et al. (2022[5]), "Coronavirus Pandemic (COVID-19)". Published online by OurWorldInData.org. Retrieved from: "https://ourworldindata.org/coronavirus".

Daily new cases are defined as "new confirmed cases of COVID-19 (7-day rolling average) per 1 000 000 people", including probable cases as reported (Ritchie et al., 2022[5]). A confirmed case of COVID-19 concerns "a person with laboratory confirmation of SARS-CoV-2 infection" (WHO, 2020[6]), regardless of possible symptoms.

Cumulative deaths are defined as "total deaths attributed to COVID-19 per 1 000 000 people" including probable deaths as reported in line with the "cause of death" classification following the WHO's International Classification of Diseases guidelines (WHO, 2022[7]). The actual number of cases and deaths caused by COVID-19 is likely to be higher than the number of confirmed cases and deaths, because of testing limitations and problems in the attribution of the cause of death. The difference between confirmed deaths and actual deaths may also vary because some countries only count hospital deaths, whilst others include deaths in homes.

References

Huang, C. et al. (2020), "Clinical features of patients infected with 2019 novel coronavirus in Wuhan, China", *The Lancet*, Vol. 395/10223, pp. 497-506, https://doi.org/10.1016/S0140-6736(20)30183-5. [1]

OECD (2022), *The impact of COVID-19 on health and health systems*, https://www.oecd.org/health/covid-19.htm. [3]

OECD/WHO (2020), *Health at a Glance: Asia/Pacific 2020: Measuring Progress Towards Universal Health Coverage*, OECD Publishing, Paris, https://doi.org/10.1787/26b007cd-en. [4]

Ritchie, H. et al. (2022), *Coronavirus Pandemic (COVID-19)*, https://ourworldindata.org/coronavirus. [5]

Roberts, D., J. Rossman and I. Jarić (2021), "Dating first cases of COVID-19", *PLOS Pathogens*, Vol. 17/6, p. e1009620, https://doi.org/10.1371/JOURNAL.PPAT.1009620. [2]

WHO (2022), *International Classification of Diseases 11th Revision - ICD-11*, https://icd.who.int/en. [7]

WHO (2020), *Coronavirus disease 2019 (COVID-19): Situation report 50*, https://www.who.int/docs/default-source/coronaviruse/situation-reports/20200310-sitrep-50-covid-19.pdf. [6]

Figure 5.16. "Pre-Omicron", COVID-19 cases peaked mid-2021 in India, Indonesia and Japan...

Daily new confirmed cases of COVID-19 per million from February 2020 until 25 December 2021

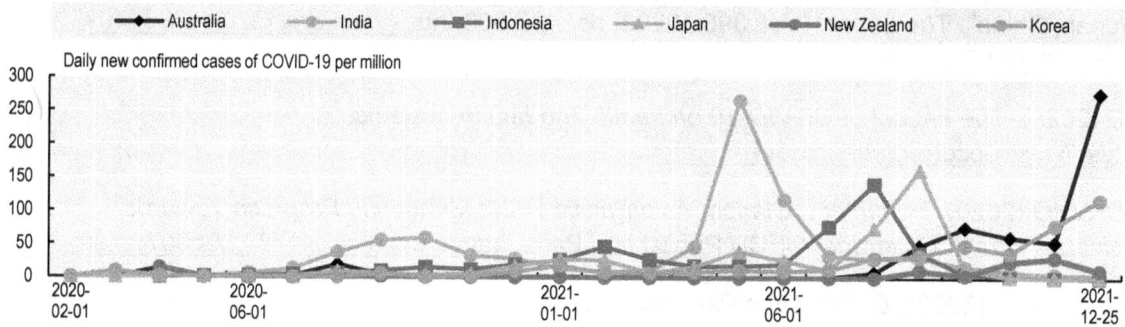

Source: Johns Hopkins University CSSE COVID-19 Data – Daily number of confirmed cases (7-day smoothed) https://ourworldindata.org/coronavirus accessed on 8 April 2022.

StatLink ᵐˢᴸ https://stat.link/u35ktl

Figure 5.17. ...while "Omicron" took cases to new heights in Australia, New Zealand and Korea in early 2022

Daily new confirmed cases of COVID-19 per million from January 2022 until April 2022

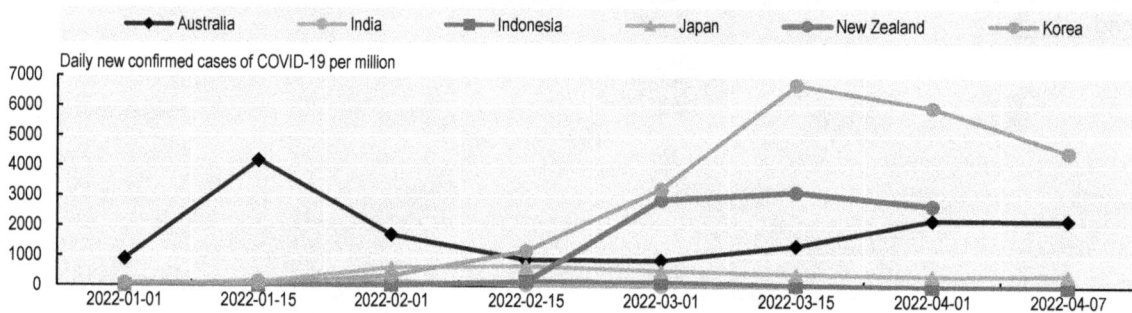

Source: Johns Hopkins University CSSE COVID-19 Data – Daily number of confirmed cases (7-day smoothed) https://ourworldindata.org/coronavirus, accessed on 8 April 2022.

StatLink ᵐˢᴸ https://stat.link/m1vcb9

Figure 5.18. By April 2020, cumulative deaths per million are highest in Indonesia, India and Korea

Cumulative deaths of COVID-19 per million in selected Asia/Pacific countries

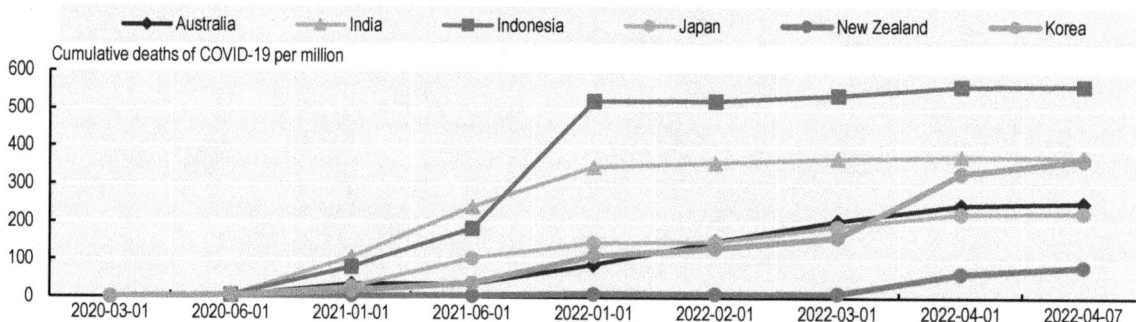

Source: Johns Hopkins University CSSE COVID-19 Data – Cumulative deaths of COVID-19 per million https://ourworldindata.org/coronavirus, accessed on 8 April 2022.

StatLink ᵐˢᴸ https://stat.link/4rc3w9

6 Social cohesion indicators

Life satisfaction

Life satisfaction represents people's subjective evaluation of their satisfaction with life as a whole. Life satisfaction is associated with good family relationships, health, living conditions and wealth as well as confidence in governance in the broader society.

People in OECD countries are more satisfied with their life than those in the Asia/Pacific region (Figure 6.1). On a scale of 1 to 10, life satisfaction scores are about 1 point higher on average across the OECD than across the Asia/Pacific region. Australians and New Zealanders report the highest life satisfaction of the countries observed, averaging a score of seven out of ten; while residents in Bangladesh, India and Sri Lanka report the lowest life-satisfaction scores in 2017/19.

On average across the Asia/Pacific region and the OECD, life satisfaction has not changed markedly since the last decade (Figure 6.1). Trends also differ across countries; for example, on average life satisfaction was low in Georgia and India in 2007/09, but while it improved in Georgia, it declined further in India in 2017/19. Life satisfaction increased in about two-thirds of the countries since 2007/09, and the increase appeared most pronounced in Georgia, Mongolia, and the Philippines.

The COVID-19 pandemic changed life around the world. On average, more than seven in ten survey-respondents declare that their life has been affected by the COVID-19 pandemic in the Asia Pacific region, compared to more than eight in ten survey respondents across the OECD area. In 2020, over 9 out of 10 survey-respondents were affected by the COVID-19 pandemic (either "a lot" or "to some extent") in Korea, Mongolia and the Philippines. Whereas less than one in two respondents were affected Lao PDR, Nepal and Tajikistan (Figure 6.2).

People in wealthy countries tend to be more satisfied with life than those in less wealthy countries (Figure 6.3). People in Uzbekistan appear to have a higher life satisfaction than what might have been expected based on their average income, but results for Australia, New Zealand on the one hand, and Bangladesh and Cambodia on the other, illustrate the relationship between average life satisfaction and prosperity.

Data and measurement

Data on life satisfaction were taken from the Gallup World Poll. The Gallup World Poll is conducted in more than 150 countries around the world based on a common questionnaire, translated into the predominant languages of each country. With few exceptions, all samples are probability based and nationally representative of the resident population aged 15 years and over in the entire country, including rural areas. While this ensures a high degree of comparability across countries, results may be affected by sampling and non-sampling error, and variation in response rates. Hence, results should be interpreted with care. These probability surveys are valid within a statistical margin of error, also called a 95% confidence interval. This means that if the survey were conducted 100 times using the exact same procedures, the margin of error would include the "true value" in 95 out of 100 surveys. Sample sizes vary across countries from 1 000 to 4 000, and as the surveys use a clustered sample design the margin of error varies by question. The margin of error declines with increasing sample size: with a sample size of 1 000, the margin of error at a 95% confidence interval is $0.98/\sqrt{\text{sample size}}$ or 3%, with a sample size of 4 000, this is 1.5%. To minimise the effect of annual fluctuations in responses related to small sample sizes, results are averaged over a three-year period, or two-year period in case of missing data. If only one observation in a three-year period is available, this finding is not reported.

The Gallup World Poll asked respondents to: "Imagine an 11-rung ladder where the bottom (0) represents the worst possible life for you and the top (10) represents the best possible life for you. On which step of the ladder do you feel you personally stand at the present time?" The main indicator used in this section is the average country score. Data are also shown by gender and broad age groups.

During the first full year of the COVID-19 pandemic, Gallup asked specific questions on how the pandemic affected respondents' lives and livelihoods. One of the question was: In general, to what extent has your own life been affected by the coronavirus situation? A lot, to Some extent or Not at all?

Figure 6.1. Life satisfaction and trends therein vary considerably across countries

Average points of life satisfaction on an 11-step ladder from 0-10

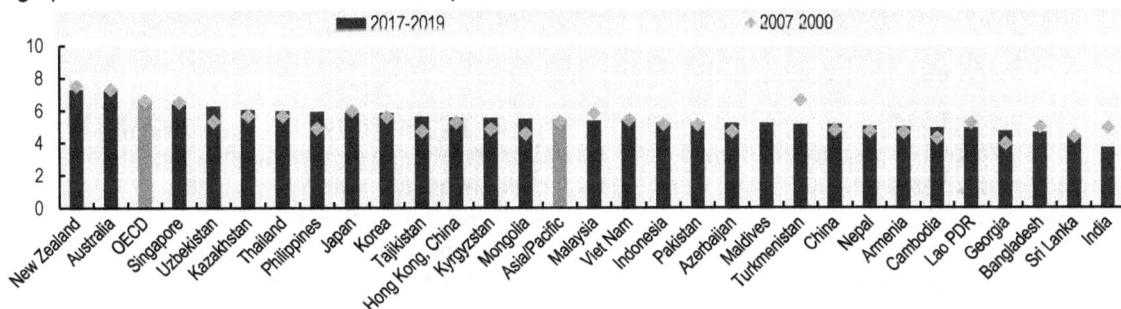

Source: Gallup (2021), Gallup World Poll, http://www.gallup.com.

StatLink ⟨S⟩ https://stat.link/nzeu73

Figure 6.2. More than 7 in 10 survey-respondents declare that their life was affected by the COVID-19 pandemic

Percentage of population declaring their life has been affected ("A lot" and "to some extent") by the coronavirus situation in 2020

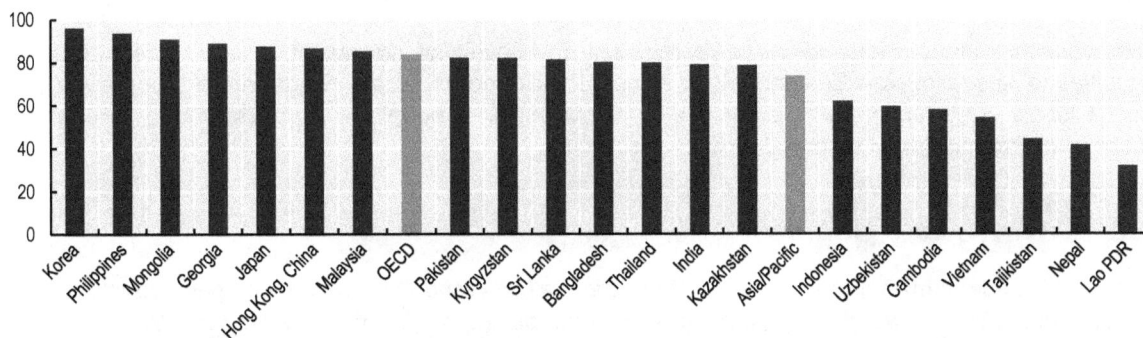

Note: Differences across countries in the dates of interviews in 2020 as well change in survey methodology (based on telephone interviewing and new weighting adjustment) may affect comparability.
Source: OECD Secretariat calculations based from Gallup (2021), Gallup World Poll, http://www.gallup.com.

StatLink ⟨S⟩ https://stat.link/wgbzja

Figure 6.3. People in wealthy countries tend to be more satisfied with life than those in less wealthy countries

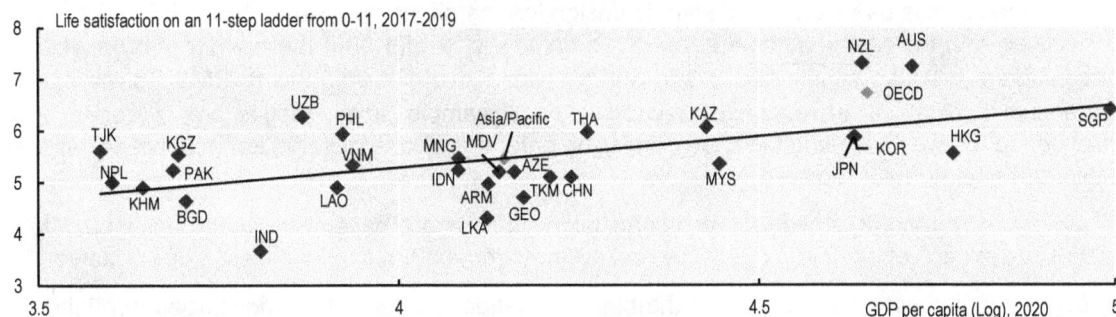

Note: GDP per capita is gross domestic product divided by midyear population. GDP is the sum of gross value added by all resident producers in the economy plus any product taxes and minus any subsidies not included in the value of the products. It is calculated without making deductions for depreciation of assets or for depletion and degradation of natural resources. Data are in current USD.
Source: Gallup (2021), Gallup World Poll, http://www.gallup.com; OECD (2021), OECD National Accounts, https://stats.oecd.org/Index.aspx?DataSetCode=NAAG; World Bank (2021), World Development Indicators, https://databank.worldbank.org/source/world-development-indicators.

StatLink ⟨S⟩ https://stat.link/5zjmie

Confidence in institutions

A cohesive society is one where citizens have confidence in national (and sub-national) level institutions and believe that social and economic institutions are not subjected to corruption. Confidence and corruption issues are dimensions that are strongly related to the societal trust.

Confidence in the national government is higher in the Asia/Pacific region than among OECD countries (Figure 6.4): Australians, Japanese, Koreans and New Zealanders have less confidence in their national governments than their Asian/Pacific peers. Confidence in national government seems lowest in Georgia, Korea and Mongolia. In about half of the countries, about 70% of the population has confidence in its national government, and this is over 90% for the populations in Singapore, Tajikistan and Uzbekistan. On average, confidence in national government is similar for youth and the rest of the adult population, but young people in Hong Kong, China have far less confidence in their government than older Hong Kong residents.

On average, across the Asia/Pacific region, confidence in the national government has changed little over the last decade, but there is a large variation in trends across countries (Figure 6.4). Trust in government declined by more than 20 percentage points in Hong Kong, China and Sri Lanka. By contrast, trust in the national government increased among the population of Indonesia, Japan and the Philippines.

Even though there is still considerable variation across countries, dispersion in the level of confidence in national government seems to have slightly declined in the Asia/Pacific region at the beginning of the pandemic (Figure 6.5). The minimum level observed in confidence in the national government increased by 10 percentage points between 2019 and 2020.

In richer countries, people tend to perceive relatively low levels of corruption in government (Figure 6.6). Communities in Australia, New Zealand, Hong Kong (China) and especially Singapore are perceived to have the lowest levels of corruption, whereas close to or over 80% of people in Kyrgyzstan and Indonesia think corruption in government is widespread.

Data and measurement

Data on confidence in institutions was taken from the Gallup World Poll, which is conducted in more than 150 countries around the world, and based on a common questionnaire, as translated into the predominant languages of each country. With few exceptions, all samples are probability based and nationally representative of the resident population aged 15 years and over in the entire country, including rural areas. While this ensures a high degree of comparability across countries, results may be affected by sampling and non-sampling error, and variation in response rates. Hence, results should be interpreted with care. These probability surveys are valid within a statistical margin of error, also called a 95% confidence interval. This means that if the survey were conducted 100 times using the exact same procedures, the margin of error would include the "true value" in 95 out of 100 surveys. Sample sizes vary across countries from 1 000 to 4 000, and as the surveys use a clustered sample design the margin of error varies by question. The margin of error declines with increasing sample size: with a sample size of 1 000, the margin of error at a 95% confidence interval is $0.98/\sqrt{\text{sample size}}$ or 3%; with a sample size of 4 000, this is 1.5%. To minimise the effect of annual fluctuations in responses related to small sample sizes, results are averaged over a three-year period, or two-year period in case of missing data. If only one observation in a three-year period is available, this finding is not reported.

Data on national government confidence and financial institutions are based on binary questions: "Do you have confidence in each of the following: In the national government? In financial institutions or banks?"

Data on corruption perception are based on the binary question: "Is corruption widespread throughout the government in this country, or not?"

Figure 6.4. Confidence in national governments is higher in the Asia/Pacific region than in OECD countries

Percentage of people responding they have confidence in their national government, 2017-19 average

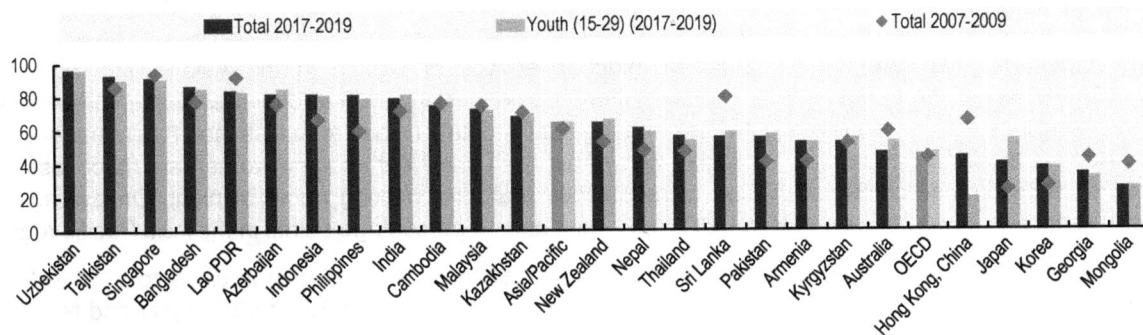

Source: Gallup (2021), Gallup World Poll, http://www.gallup.com; World Bank (2021), World Development Indicators, https://databank.worldbank.org/source/world-development-indicators.

StatLink ᵐˢ▣ https://stat.link/v72lhs

Figure 6.5. Minimum level of confidence in national government increased in Asia/Pacific at the beginning of the pandemic

Percentage of people responding they have confidence in their national government, 2019 and 2020

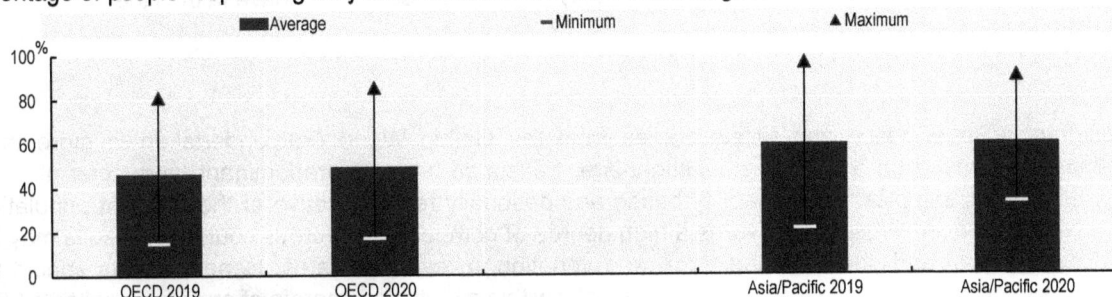

Note: Data refer to countries for which data are available for both years.
Source: Gallup (2021), Gallup World Poll, http://www.gallup.com.

StatLink ᵐˢ▣ https://stat.link/m4pegl

Figure 6.6. Corruption is perceived to be lower in richer countries

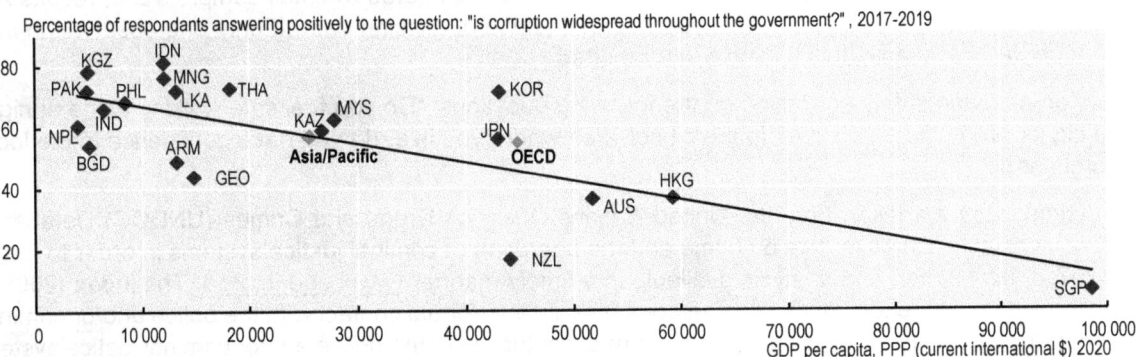

Source: Gallup (2021), Gallup World Poll, http://www.gallup.com; OECD (2021), OECD National Accounts, https://stats.oecd.org/Index.aspx?DataSetCode=NAAG; World Bank (2021), World Development Indicators, https://databank.worldbank.org/source/world-development-indicators.

StatLink ᵐˢ▣ https://stat.link/soni8j

Trust and safety

Trust and safety in a society reflect how people feel that their freedom of movement and their property are protected. A high level of personal trust and safety can promote openness and transparency in society, social interaction and cohesion.

People, in general, feel safe walking alone at night: over 70% of people in the Asia/Pacific region and OECD countries would agree (Figure 6.7). However, there is a gender gap as in all countries women are less likely to report feeling safe walking alone at night. The gender gap accounts for close to or less than 5 percentage points in Hong Kong (China), Singapore and Tajikistan, while Australian and New Zealand women are much less likely (by around 30 percentage points) than men to report they feel safe walking home at night. On average, the difference is about 15 percentage points in OECD countries and 13 percentage points in the Asia/Pacific region.

Almost 96% of Singaporeans feel comfortable being on the street at night, which is close to 90% in China, Tajikistan and Turkmenistan. By contrast, less than 60% of the population in Bhutan, Malaysia and Nepal feel safe walking home at night. (Figure 6.7).

The crime rate has decreased in some countries in the Asia/Pacific region (Figure 6.8): on average the reported crime rates in countries for which data are available have decreased by about 30 percentage points since 2008. However, this masks considerable variation in country experiences; reported crime rates declined significantly in New Zealand and Sri Lanka since 2008 whereas they increased most in Armenia, India and Kazakhstan.

Confidence in law enforcement is relatively high overall (Figure 6.9). Over 70% of the population in the Asia/Pacific region and OECD countries trust the local police. This proportion is highest at over 85% of respondents in Indonesia, Singapore and Uzbekistan. Less than 60% of respondents in Armenia trust their local police, but this is nowhere as low as in Kyrgyzstan and Pakistan where only half of the respondents have faith in the police.

Data and measurement

Data on trust in local police and safety comes from the Gallup World Poll undertaken in more than 150 countries as based on a common questionnaire, translated into the predominant languages of each country. In general, samples are probability based and nationally representative of the resident population aged 15 years and over. While this ensures a high degree of comparability across countries, results may be affected by sampling and non-sampling error, and variation in response rates. Hence, results should be interpreted with care. These probability surveys are valid within a statistical margin of error, also called a 95% confidence interval. This means that if the survey were conducted 100 times using the exact same procedures, the margin of error would include the "true value" in 95 out of 100 surveys. Sample sizes vary across countries from 1 000 to 4 000, and as the surveys use a clustered sample design the margin of error varies by question. The margin of error declines with increasing sample size: with a sample size of 1 000, the margin of error at a 95% confidence interval is $0.98/\sqrt{\text{sample size}}$ or 3%, with a sample size of 4 000, this is 1.5%. To minimise the effect of annual fluctuations in responses related to small sample sizes, results are averaged over a three-year period, or two-year period in case of missing data. If only one observation in a three-year period is available, this finding is not reported.

Indicators on trust and safety are based on the following questions: "Do you feel safe walking alone at night or in the city or area where you live? In the city or area where you live, do you have confidence in the local police force, or not?"

Data on crime rates are taken from the United Nations Office on Drugs and Crimes (UNDOC) Database. UNODC collects administrative data on crime and the operation of criminal justice systems in order to make policy-relevant information and analysis available in a timely manner (www.unodc.org/). The index (2008 = 100) concerns data on the total number of persons brought into formal contact with the police and/or criminal justice system, all crimes have taken together. "Formal contact" with the police and/or criminal justice system may include persons suspected, arrested or cautioned. Cross-national comparisons should be interpreted with care because of the differences that exist between the legal definitions of offences in countries or the different methods of counting and recording offences.

Figure 6.7. Women feel less secure walking alone at night than men

Share of people responding they feel safe walking alone at night in the city or area where they live, 2017-19

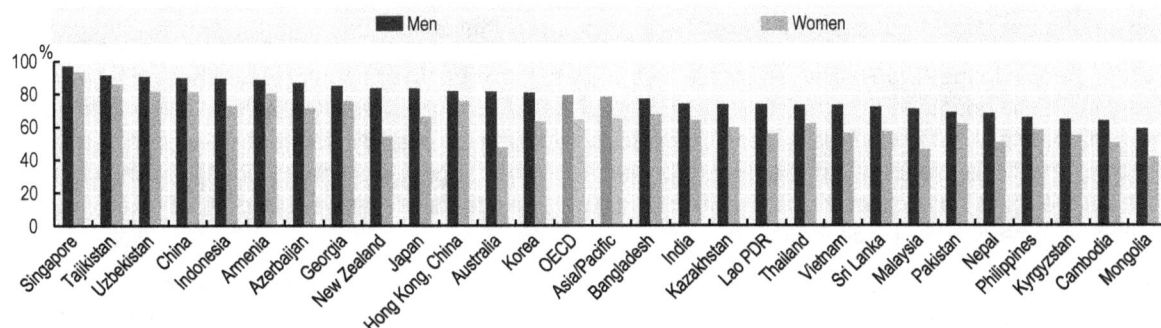

Source: Gallup (2021), Gallup World Poll, http://www.gallup.com.

StatLink https://stat.link/3z7a1o

Figure 6.8. Crime declined in some countries over the last decade

Total persons per 100 000 population brought into formal contact with the police and/or criminal justice system in 2018 or nearest year, all crimes, index 100 in 2008

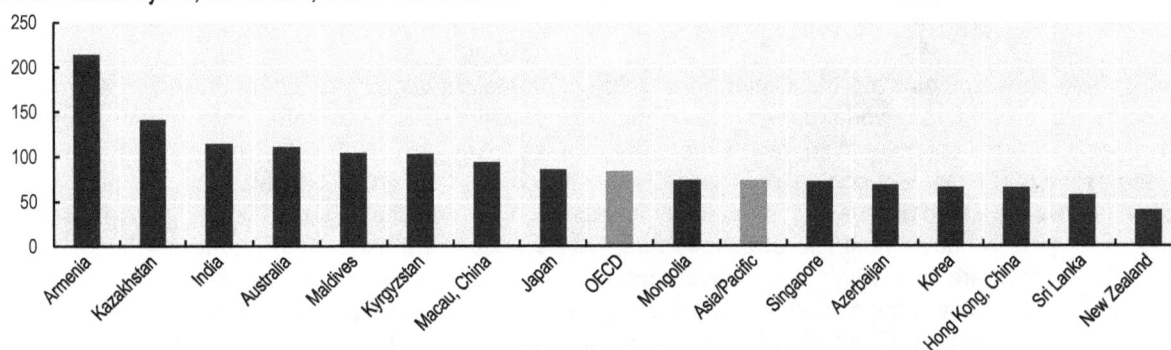

Note: Instead of 2018, data refer to 2013 for India and Maldives, 2015 for Kazakhstan, 2016 for Japan and Sri Lanka, and 2017 for Australia.
Source: United Nations Office on Drugs and Crimes (UNDOC) (2021), www.unodc.org.

StatLink https://stat.link/kxahlo

Figure 6.9. Confidence in the local police remains high

Share of people responding they have confidence in the local police, 2017-19

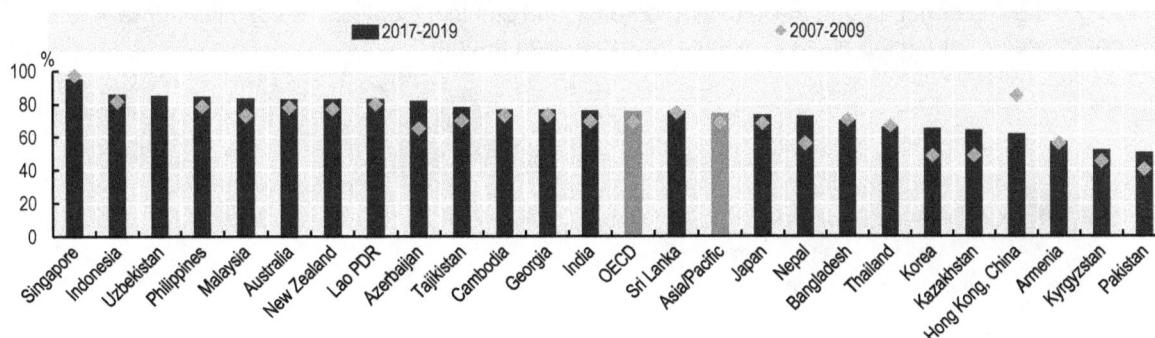

Source: Gallup (2021), Gallup World Poll, http://www.gallup.com.

StatLink https://stat.link/ghdsov

Tolerance

The degree of community acceptance of minority groups is a measurable dimension of social cohesion. Acceptance of three such groups is considered here: migrants, ethnic minorities and gay and lesbian people.

On average, people in the Asia/Pacific region are less likely to think that their country welcomes immigrants than their peers in OECD countries (Figure 6.10). Over 85% of Australians and New Zealanders respond affirmative when asked whether their country is a good place to live for immigrants. By contrast, less than a quarter of Cambodians and Malaysians say the same (Figure 6.10). The biggest decline in positive sentiment since 2007/2009 appears to have taken place in Cambodia, while residents of Pakistan and Uzbekistan think their country has become a better place for immigrants.

On average across the Asia/Pacific and OECD countries at least two-thirds of the population consider their country tolerant towards ethnic minorities (Figure 6.11). Overall perception of tolerance towards ethnic minorities increased by more than 10 percentage points over the last decade in the Asia/Pacific region. The largest increases were observed in Cambodia, Indonesia and Pakistan.

OECD countries appear on average to be more tolerant of gays and lesbians than countries in the Asia/Pacific region (Figure 6.12). Nepal, New Zealand and Australia record the highest perceived tolerance levels followed by the Philippines and Hong Kong (China). Only less than 5% of the population in Armenia and Azerbaijan report that their country is a good place to live for gays and lesbians.

Data and measurement

Data on tolerance comes from the Gallup World Poll. The Gallup World Poll is conducted in more than 150 countries around the world based on a common questionnaire, translated into the predominant languages of each country. With few exceptions, all samples are probability based and nationally representative of the resident population aged 15 years and over in the entire country, including rural areas. While this ensures a high degree of comparability across countries, results may be affected by sampling and non-sampling error, and variation in response rates. Hence, results should be interpreted with care. These probability surveys are valid within a statistical margin of error, also called a 95% confidence interval. This means that if the survey is conducted 100 times using the exact same procedures, the margin of error would include the "true value" in 95 out of 100 surveys. Sample sizes vary across countries from 1 000 to 4 000, and as the surveys use a clustered sample design the margin of error varies by question. The margin of error declines with increasing sample size: with a sample size of 1 000, the margin of error at a 95% confidence interval is $0.98/\sqrt{\text{sample size}}$ or 3%; with a sample size of 4 000, this is 1.5%. To minimise the effect of annual fluctuations in responses related to small sample sizes, results are averaged over a three-year period, or two-year period in case of missing data. If only one observation in a three-year period is available, this finding is not reported.

The results presented in this indicator are based on the following questions: "Is the city or area where you live a good place or not a good place to live for immigrants from other countries? Is the city or area where you live a good place or not a good place to live for racial and ethnic minorities? Is the city or area where you live a good place or not a good place to live for gay or lesbian people?"

77

Figure 6.10. OECD countries are more likely to think their society is a good place to live for immigrants than economies in the Asia/Pacific region

Share of people who think that the city or area where they live is a good place to live for immigrants from other countries

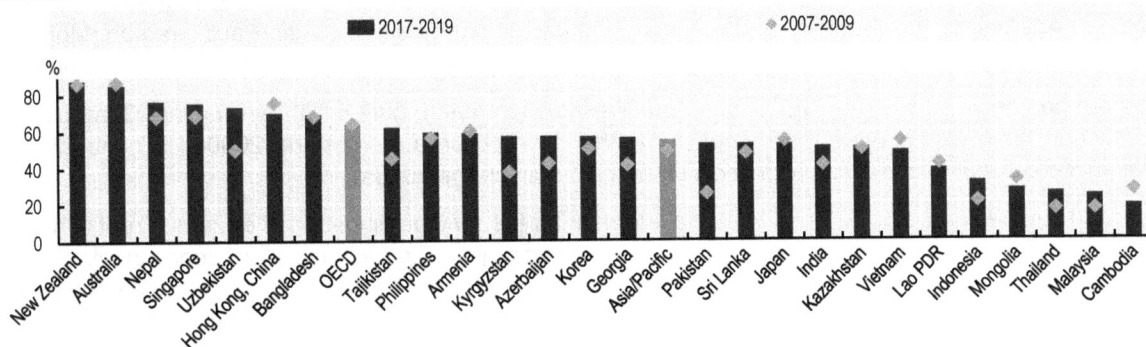

Source: Gallup (2021), Gallup World Poll, http://www.gallup.com.

StatLink ᐧᐧ https://stat.link/1b87p0

Figure 6.11. Variation in perceived tolerance for ethnic minorities

Share of people who think that the city or area where they live is a good place to live for racial and ethnic minorities

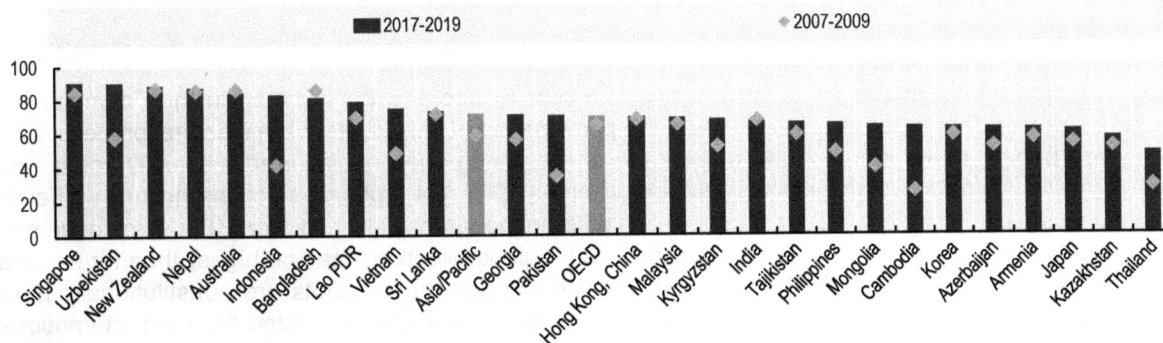

Source: Gallup (2021), Gallup World Poll, http://www.gallup.com.

StatLink ᐧᐧ https://stat.link/n4rj3y

Figure 6.12. Perceived tolerance for gays and lesbians increased in OECD and Asia/Pacific countries over the last decade

Share of people who think that the city or area where they live is a good place to live for gay or lesbian people

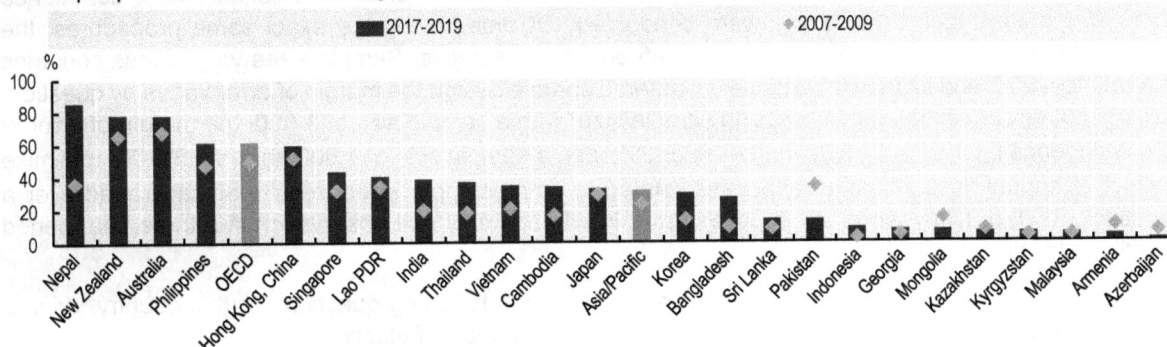

Source: Gallup (2021), Gallup World Poll, http://www.gallup.com.

StatLink ᐧᐧ https://stat.link/9ke87z

SOCIETY AT A GLANCE: ASIA/PACIFIC 2022 © OECD 2022

Voting

A high voter turnout is a sign that a country's political system enjoys a strong degree of participation. Voter turnout rates vary hugely across the region (Figure 6.13). Over nine in every ten people turn out to vote in parliamentary elections in Papua New Guinea, Timor-Leste and Viet Nam, compared to less than one in every two people in Azerbaijan, Fiji, Georgia, and Pakistan, the lowest turnouts in the Asia/Pacific region. More than half of the eligible population votes in all other countries for data on voter turnout in parliamentary elections.

Voter turnout has declined in some OECD and Asia/Pacific countries (Figure 6.13). Azerbaijan, Cambodia, Fiji and Uzbekistan have experienced the sharpest decline in voter turnout since the 2000s. In contrast, voter participation increased most in Singapore and Turkmenistan since the 2000s.

Confidence in the electoral process is an essential element for the civic participation of citizens. Trust in honesty of elections increased in most countries across the Asia/Pacific region (Figure 6.14). Confidence in fair elections increased most in Armenia, India, Indonesia and the Philippines (by about or more than 20 percentage points); while the largest decline in trust in the election process was observed in Hong Kong, China.

In general, people who live in countries with higher trust in elections also appear to have strong confidence in the national government across the Asia/Pacific region and vice versa (Figure 6.15). India, Indonesia and Singapore tend to report high trust in elections and high confidence in national government while Georgia and Mongolia report limited confidence in government and election processes. However, the high trust in elections is not always associated with confidence in the national government. More than 70% of Azerbaijanis and Kazakhs report their trust in the national government, but only one in two trusts the election process (Figure 6.15).

Data and measurement

Voting in national parliamentary elections is one indicator of people's participation in their community's national life. The indicator used here to measure the participation of individuals in the electoral process is the "Voting age population turnout", i.e. the percentage of the voting age population that actually voted – as available from administrative records of member countries. Different types of elections occur in different countries according to their institutional structure and different geographical jurisdictions. For some countries, it should be noted, turnout for presidential elections and regional elections may be higher than for national parliamentary elections, perhaps because those elected through these ballots are constitutionally more important for how those countries are run. Data about voter turnout were extracted from the international database managed by the Institute for Democratic and Electoral Assistance (IDEA).

Data on confidence in "fairness of elections" were taken from the Gallup World Poll. The Gallup World Poll is conducted in more than 150 countries around the world based on a common questionnaire, translated into the predominant languages of each country. With few exceptions, all samples are probability based and nationally representative of the resident population aged 15 years and over in the entire country, including rural areas. While this ensures a high degree of comparability across countries, results may be affected by sampling and non-sampling error, and variation in response rates. Hence, results should be interpreted with care. These probability surveys are valid within a statistical margin of error, also called a 95% confidence interval. This means that if the survey were conducted 100 times using the exact same procedures, the margin of error would include the "true value" in 95 out of 100 surveys. Sample sizes vary across countries from 1 000 to 4 000, and as the surveys use a clustered sample design the margin of error varies by question. The margin of error declines with increasing sample size: with a sample size of 1 000, the margin of error at a 95% confidence interval is $0.98/\sqrt{\text{sample size}}$ or 3%; with a sample size of 4 000, this is 1.5%. To minimise the effect of annual fluctuations in responses related to small sample sizes, results are averaged over a three-year period, or two-year period in case of missing data. If only one observation in a three-year period is available, this finding is not reported.

Data on confidence in the fairness of elections is based on the following question: "In this country, do you have confidence in each of the following, or not? How about honesty of elections?"

Figure 6.13. Electoral participation varies greatly across countries

Voting age population turnout at most recent parliamentary elections (%)

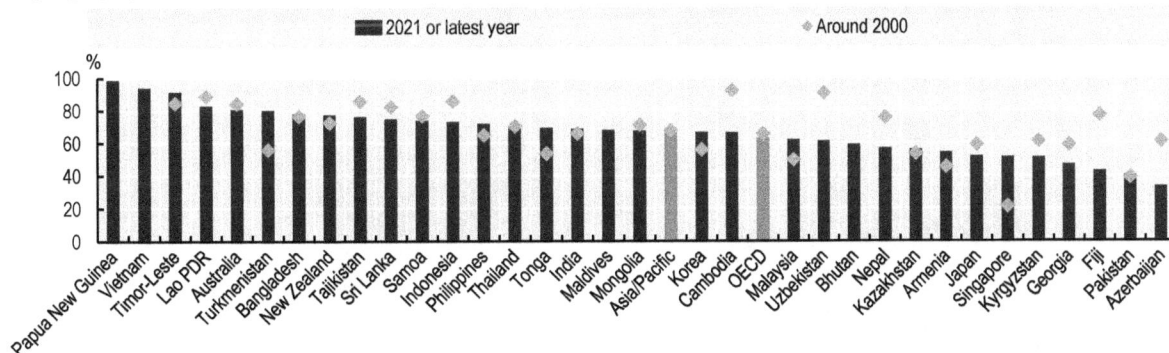

Note: Voting age population turnout, i.e. the percentage of the voting age population that actually voted – as available from administrative records of member countries.
Source: Institute for Democratic and Electoral Assistance (IDEA) (2021), www.idea.int/.

StatLink ᵐˢᴾ https://stat.link/ml3irs

Figure 6.14. Confidence in fairness of elections generally increased in the Asia Pacific region

Share of people responding they have confidence in fairness of elections

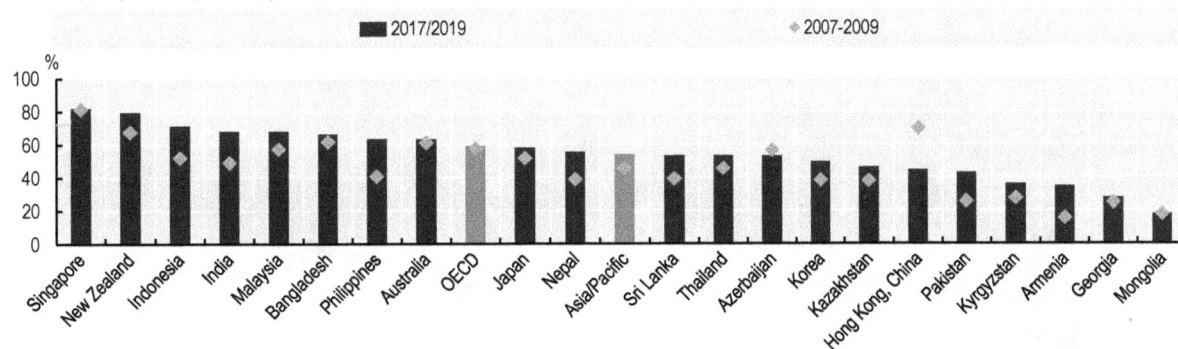

Source: Gallup (2021), Gallup World Poll, http://www.gallup.com.

StatLink ᵐˢᴾ https://stat.link/foz9ud

Figure 6.15. People who live in countries with high confidence in elections tend to report high trust in national government

Percentage of confidence in national government and elections, 2017-19

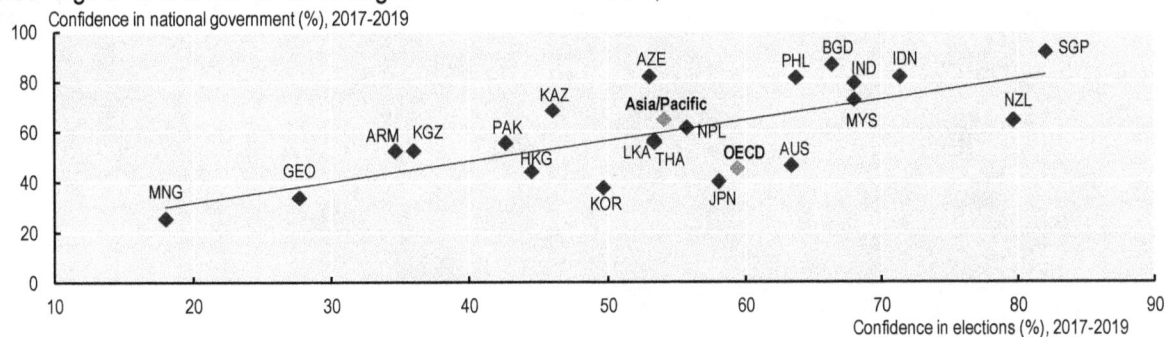

Source: Gallup (2021), Gallup World Poll, http://www.gallup.com.

StatLink ᵐˢᴾ https://stat.link/0r4wyz

www.ingramcontent.com/pod-product-compliance
Lightning Source LLC
Chambersburg PA
CBHW080339270326
41927CB00014B/3292